We spotted two MiGs, higher than we were, that obviously didn't see us. All of a sudden the lead MiG's wing dropped, the nose came around and I could feel the hair at the base of my neck try to stand up. I realized there, in that moment of time, I saw him, he saw me and one of us was not going home. The world's most dangerous game had begun.

We closed rapidly, me climbing and the MiG turning and diving slightly. We passed within a few hundred yards—our combined speeds about 1,000 miles per hour. I was anxious, eager, excited and scared. How good was the MiG-15? All I knew was what I had been told. Now I was about to find out for myself.

"CHECK SIX"
A Fighter Pilot Looks Back

Major General
F. C. "Boots" Blesse,
USAF (Ret.)

IVY BOOKS • NEW YORK

Ivy Books
Published by Ballantine Books
Copyright © 1987 by F. C. Blesse

Library of Congress Catalog Card Number: 87-32635

ISBN 0-8041-0927-3

This edition published by arrangement with Champlin Fighter Museum Press

Manufactured in the United States of America

First Ballantine Books Edition: February 1992

Dedication

This book is dedicated to the United States Air Force. I lived it, I loved it, and no one had a better time in it than I did. Without the Air Force, I would have missed flying the best fighter aircraft the world had to offer at the time, and I would never have met the many men and women who so enriched my life. I am also deeply indebted to my wife, Betty, without whose understanding, patience, and constant encouragement this book would have never been written.

Table of Contents

Preface

I would like to say a word or two about the title. "Check Six" is a slang expression known to all fighter pilots; it says check behind you (the six o'clock position) because that is where you are most vulnerable in a fighter. Through the years the expression came to be used in place of "take care of yourself," "watch the razor in the dark," "don't take any wooden nickels," or other such phrases that throw a friendly piece of advice your way on departure. A fighter pilot who fails to check six regularly in combat will in all probability become another name on the casualty list.

The story I have told is as I remember it, since it was done without notes to which I could refer. It is possible a date or name could have been used in error; if so, my apologies. Some names have been omitted or changed intentionally to prevent simply adding interest at someone else's expense.

If I had to describe my own efforts in writing *"Check Six,"* I would have to call it a biographical novel because it really is a story—a true story of ambition, fun, anxiety, aggression, frustration, death, sorrow, and a thousand other descriptive words known only to those who have zoomed their aircraft to the stars and "touched the face of God" in the process.

Acknowledgments

I extend my thanks and appreciation to the following people for their help in getting this story into its final form:

For typing and computer reproduction work: Mrs. Linda Messina

For editing and reviewing:

Barrett Tillman
Doug Champlin
Dr. Jeff Ethell
Col. Remo Nicoli
Gordon Ochenrider

Rob Suthann
Bonnie Sansonetti
Ralph Lowe
Melanie D. Blesse
Mrs. Betty Blesse

For contributing comments and data:

Maj. Gen. Fred Haeffner
Brig. Gen. Jay Hubbard
Lt. Col. John Taylor
Col. William Hawkins
Mr. Jim Kumph
Col. Wilbur Grumbles
Col. Walt Kross
Mr. "Skosh" Littlefield
Brig. Gen. Robin Olds
Brig. Gen. Robbie Risner
Col. Edward Mason
Col. Billy Hovde
Mrs. Kay Chandler

Col. Houston Tuel
Col. Walker Mahurin
Col. Bob Janca
Col. Bruce Hinton
Mr. John Kumph
Lt. Gen. Charles Cleveland
Col. Carl Weaver
Maj. Gen. F. L. Smith
Col. Lou Green
Mr. William Kennedy
Col. James Raebel
Col. Jerry Brown
Mr. Buck Haynes
Gen. James Allen

CHAPTER 1

MGM Hotel, Las Vegas, 21 November 1980

"Honey, wake up! Wake up! I smell smoke!"

I struggled to bring myself around, but it wasn't easy. When I finally got my eyes open, I realized they were burning, and it wasn't because we had been out late last night, even though we had. Betty was right about one thing—she did smell smoke. I jumped out of bed and ran to the door. When I opened it, thick, acrid smoke rolled in like a wall of water. I slammed the door and called to Betty, "Honey, call the desk and see what's going on. We have a hell of a problem up here!"

"I did that and the lines are dead," she shouted. From that moment we were on our own—three hours in the loneliest world I have ever been in.

I have been in all kinds of tight spots—emergencies become a part of your life when you spend thirty years flying fighter aircraft. They simply appear now and then and you deal with them, but this was different. This wasn't dashing over a well-defended target for eight minutes or so. This was sustained pressure caused by a set of circumstances you didn't understand, creating problems for which you had no memorized solutions.

As the room filled with smoke, we had to use the balcony to be able to breathe. The smoke got worse. At first, from our twenty-fifth-floor room, we could see people in other parts of the building, but as the smoke became thicker, our world began to close in on us. It wasn't long before it became obvious that at best it was a toss-up as to whether or not we would get off this balcony alive.

My mind began to wander a bit. We had done all we could; the rest would just have to happen. But I couldn't believe, after all my years flying—crashes, parachute jumps, fires, combat— that the good Lord had decided this was the way I was to go. He could have taken me at his leisure. Why not the night I fell asleep driving my dad's car home from a date? A 500-pound transformer hung by a shredded line above the wrecked '37 Chevy. All it had to do was fall. Why did He keep me from taking that final step into a whirling propeller when I was night-flying as a cadet at West Point? And, through the fighter years, surely He could have pulled the final string a dozen times or more. My P-51 could just as easily have burned when I hit that truck while landing on a grass field in Korea. The sharks were all over the place the day I jumped out of that P-47 into the East China Sea; for fifteen minutes they had their chance. Why not the day I ejected from the F-86 over Korea? It's so easy to tangle a chute or fail to separate from the seat during ejection. I went through five aircrafts during a year in Vietnam. Any one of those times He could have decided to end it, but He didn't! At that moment I took encouragement from the fact that God had spared me in twenty or thirty other brushes with death and that He wouldn't cook me in a hotel fire and send me off to fighter-pilot's heaven like a barbecued hot dog.

I was jolted back to reality when Betty spoke to me. I don't recall what she said. I just remember I was struck by her courage—no tears, no *why me*'s—just "What do you want me to do next?" I wondered again, would we make it? At that moment only He knew.

CHAPTER 2

The Early Years

Although I was born in the Panama Canal Zone, 22 August 1921, the first things I can remember had to do with Carlisle Barracks, Pennsylvania. Dad was a doctor in the Army, assigned there in 1925 as a student at the Medical Field Service School. At the end of the one-year course he was kept on as an instructor for four more years.

Since I was only nine when we left, I don't remember a great deal about Carlisle. I do recall I hit my first golf ball there. Dad gave me an old mashie (you'd know it as a five-iron) which he had cut down to my size. I'll never forget hitting balls on the parade ground in the evening. Now and then came that perfect hit, dead in the sweet spot, and I was always amazed at how far the ball would go when it was hit just right. I was to love that feeling the rest of my life to the extent of considering a career in professional golf, then rejecting it for the privilege of flying for Uncle Sam.

Actually, I remember other things about Carlisle—like going through long, covered, wooden bridges to get to Linder's Golf Club where Dad and Mom played. In the summer the Army held maneuvers in that area, and we would all go out there on the weekend to see Dad. I remember band concerts on the post on hot summer evenings and lots of fireflies which we caught and imprisoned in our mason jars. I remember cold

3

winters and what seemed like terribly long walks from the only good sledding hill available. I recall a hailstorm with stones the size of baseballs. They ruined every car that wasn't under cover—dents in the metal and holes in the roof. I stored a bucket full of them in the icebox till Mom made me throw them out a week or so later.

When I was a little tyke I used to put my feet in Dad's shoes and shuffle into the living room for all to see. The shoes were so large on me they looked like boots, and after a while it was, "Here come the boots again." That was shortened to just plain Boots, and the name stuck.

I had a pal, Sandy Sandrock. We went everywhere together. But even friends fight, and I can still see and hear soldiers in the barracks taking sides and rooting for one or the other as we went at it.

I'll never forget the Lothrop family, at least four boys, all of whom went to West Point. When they came home at Christmas in their uniforms, they were a sight to behold. The women made over them, the girls were in awe, and we younger ones took it all in. The feeling I got was that someday I would like to be accepted that way. That uniform was proof you could hack it. Not to be taken lightly was the roosterlike effect the sons had on their father. It would be nice to have your father feel that way about you. I'm sure the Lothrop boys were directly responsible for planting the West Point seed in me. God, they were something!

And there was a military bakery where Sandy and I used to go for a handout. Is there anything better than warm, fresh-baked bread?

I remember breaking my arm in Carlisle in 1929, trying to play Tarzan on some parallel bars. Eight weeks in a cast, with a couple of fights and using it as a baseball bat—that damn thing caused me a lot of trouble.

Summer in Carlisle was special. Dad and Mom rented a cabin on Lake Michigan and that was our yearly vacation.

Fishing from the rowboat, the great trails in the woods, and cooking the fish in the evening are all memories that will linger till the shadows are long and narrow for me. One day I caught a fishhook in my leg above the knee. Dad had to cut it out after I walked about a half mile back to the cabin. That one I would just as soon forget.

In the summer of 1930, Dad got orders to Command and General Staff School at Fort Leavenworth, Kansas. New place, new friends, new house—the familiar pattern of service life every two or three years.

Mom had been having terrible headaches, so she was operated on shortly after we got to Leavenworth. Something went wrong and she died 6 October 1930, leaving Dad with thirteen- and eleven-year-old daughters and a nine-year-old son. He came back early that morning and told us. It didn't sink in for an hour or more, but I can remember crawling under the steps of our apartment building at 326 Donovan Avenue and crying my heart out for a couple of hours.

Fort Leavenworth was a well-organized post about four or five times the size of Carlisle. For the kids, it was divided into different sections, so we had Cub Scout, Boy Scout, and Girl Scout troops in each section. I was in one of the two packs of Cub Scouts, because there were too many kids to handle in just one. Our primary form of pack vs. pack competition was sports. I was on the boxing team, then played football when I was ten and eleven with all the equipment—cleats, shoulder pads, and everything. We played regularly scheduled games against all the other Cub Scout teams in the area. There was also baseball and swimming. I got a pin for being the best boxer, and I was really proud of that thing. I still have it somewhere.

At Leavenworth, Dad attended school every night by radio. The Command and Staff School broadcast *La Paloma*, and when that happened everybody had to be quiet so he could listen and take notes. The program provided a whole evening's worth of Spanish, so he had to listen carefully. No doubt that was a real challenge with a house full of young kids who had bundles of excess energy.

Our top-floor apartment in the big building on Donovan Avenue was next to the polo field. The post also had the first regulation-size golf course I had the opportunity of playing. The first day Dad took me out in 1930, he made a hole in one. Until the summer of 1972 I'd never been with anyone else who made one. Not only was I really proud of him, but Dad got all kinds of stuff for the feat—cases of soft drinks, whiskey, golf goodies. I don't remember playing much golf then, but I sure remember that day.

My first interest in flying also came at Fort Leavenworth. There was a Captain Harvey in the Air Corps, a branch of the Army then, who lived in the apartment across from us. He was a pilot and I talked to him quite a bit, particularly about "pursuit planes," as they were called then. There was an airfield on the post, but I never got a flight. At times I'd go down to the field and often see the mass of twisted metal, wings, and propellers in a big heap deposited behind the hangar. I knew only enough to be interested, not scared.

I had my first girlfriend at Leavenworth: Margaret, a captain's daughter. Nothing serious, except that I had a crush on her and noticed that girls were a little different from boys. Like golf, that stuck with me for the rest of my life, sometimes to my detriment. Little did I know the effect some special ladies would have on my life.

As I was to learn, not only in my youth but during my own career, military families move incessantly. We hadn't been in Kansas for two years when, in 1932, the family moved to Washington, D.C.

In Washington, Dad rented a house on Aspen Street down the block from the entrance to Walter Reed Army Hospital. He was not assigned to the hospital, but worked in a building on Constitution Avenue doing medical planning. I liked Washington and went to school in Tacoma Park. We had good friends, lots of athletics, marble tournaments, and I was on the school patrol. Every morning I would report to a particular corner and help kids cross the street. Without my lofty job, there was the lurking danger they'd be hit by cars. Looking back on it, I enjoyed wearing the white belt and badge more than the job. I never gave enough of myself on things like that. I'd do what I was supposed to do but it never inspired me to become captain of the patrol. I was simply content to be there.

To begin seventh grade I was transferred to Paul Junior High School where I remember baseball games and track meets . . . and breaking my arm, in the same way I had at Carlisle, on a set of parallel bars while waiting for the school bus. Girls were becoming increasingly important. I wasn't a social whiz but enjoyed being with girls and usually had one that I was interested in. Rhoda was one of my favorites in Washington, D.C. Her father was in the Army, too, and her brother, Bud, about five years older, went to West Point. A blond, good-looking guy, he really impressed me. It was obvious that my future was being influenced by these older kids who had made it to the Military Academy.

Watching my sisters, June and Mick, date, I followed suit with Rhoda. Our being together was a strong friendship more than anything else—bike riding, tennis, and movies primarily.

The post pool had a lifeguard named Smitty who was in the Army. He and several others encouraged the kids to swim by having a summer-long marathon race. You had to swim at least ten laps at a time to count toward the goal of swimming twenty-one miles. There was a big board with your name on it and many little squares. Every time you swam over ten laps, you came in and marked on the board with a pencil that you had so many more laps to go. It was all marked out for the number of laps per mile and believe me, it took all summer to do it. Like the Boy Scouts, you had to commit yourself to it if you were going to do any good. Though I worked hard, I didn't quite finish—I got nineteen miles or so, but there was only one kid who made the full twenty-one miles. I think I came in third.

Golf remained a vague but interesting part of my life—something I never tired of. Dad belonged to the Army-Navy Country Club in Virginia, and on Sundays we'd go with him—swimming pool, putting greens, great food. My sisters would bring their boyfriends along and go swimming while I played golf in the afternoon. By the time we left Washington, I was barely fifteen and shooting around 40 on nine holes, but I never practiced enough to get a glimpse of my capabilities.

Dad was getting his own life back to normal and in 1936 he married again. I liked Lucy Kuhn and I thought Luddy, as she was nicknamed, was a fine person. She made it a point to do some very nice things for me. The marriage, however, caused a big ruckus with my two sisters—primarily June, who didn't get along with her and who never really got over it. Mick, being younger, had a better attitude and, after some considerable time, she and Luddy became good friends.

By October 1936, we were moving again. We boarded the old Army transport *Grant*, sailed through the Panama Canal to San Francisco and Hawaii, and then were off to new adventures and friends in the Philippine Islands.

Manila was a splendid city in the fall of 1936—nice roads, beautiful buildings, good people. But when you left the Manila area, except to a prominent destination, the roads were poor and the buildings turned into Nepa huts where people had lived for centuries. They were good people—friendly, happy, and, for the most part, honest and hardworking. It was typically tropic—showers and sunshine alternating throughout most of the day, except during the dry season (March, April, and May). There was a wonderful transportation system—a fleet of small jeep-like vehicles with room for four people sitting in the back in the open behind the driver—two on each side facing each other. You flagged him down, paid your nickel, and rode as far as he went. They ran continuously on Rizal Avenue and Dewey Boulevard. Taxis were available if you didn't mind risking a heart attack. The first horn to blow coming into the intersection had the right of way and there were lots of bluffers.

The Manila Hotel and the Army-Navy Club seemed to be the mainstays in town, while life elsewhere revolved around the American bases scattered throughout the island of Luzon. In 1936, Clark Field was a very small airfield near Fort Stotsenberg, which was a large post sixty miles north of Manila. Nichols Field, near Manila, housed most of our good aircraft although there were several other airfields that increased in importance as war with Japan drew closer. Cavite Naval Base and Corregidor added more color and were destined to become household words that in 1936 no one in the States had ever heard of.

My teenage years in the Philippines were great fun. Fort McKinley kids went to school from seven A.M. until noon. So, every afternoon about one o'clock I was out on the golf course, until we left in late 1939. My golf matured, and by the time I had been there about a year I was playing with a scratch handicap in tournaments all over the islands. I won the Junior Philippine Department Championship in 1937, 1938, and 1939, and played in the Philippine Open one year, qualifying third.

Three things were important to me during this wonderful time. The first was Kay, the girl I started dating. Later we became serious and remained so for a long time. Next came athletics, and third was school. Each influenced me considerably.

My primary objective in school was to avoid flunking and not get any Ds in the process. Like most kids, I wrote love notes, skipped school, and did whatever I wanted to instead of knuckling down. Matter of fact, I skipped a lot of school I shouldn't have. I never did get in much trouble, and when I had to, I'd study hard enough and long enough to pass, but I wasn't doing anything academically.

Golf was my primary form of athletics. One of the biggest influences on me at the time was Gene Sarazen, who came to the Philippines in 1938, a year after he won the Masters, for an exhibition match at Fort McKinley. Three golfers in the club were chosen to play with him, and I happened to be one. I guess it was unusual for a kid my age to have a scratch handicap.

There seemed to be a couple thousand people walking around that afternoon. Looking back, I feel very pleased at what I was able to do at that age, though I didn't feel the pressure of a three-foot putt like I do now. Sarazen broke the course record by one stroke with a 65. That was one round of golf I'll never forget. All of us played well—two of us shot in the 60s and the other shot a 70.

Afterwards, I had the opportunity to talk to Mr. Sarazen, and he asked me what I had in mind for a life's work. I told him that up until the last year or so I had never really thought about anything other than going to West Point and then becoming a fighter pilot. Recently, a lot of folks had been suggesting a career in professional golf would be a natural for me. We talked about it at some length and, when asked what he thought, he said, "I'll give you my opinion based on my own life. When you get out there and start competing with all these guys, you'll find they're all pretty good, too. There are no assurances that you're going to win, and when you have to win to eat, believe me, golf loses a good bit of its luster. There's every reason to believe you'd have as good a chance as anyone, but it isn't all peaches and cream. I believe I'd go on to West Point, get my degree, and then become a fighter pilot if that's what you want to do in life. Use golf as a vent for your frustrations and as a way of meeting people. You'll find as you go through life that you'll meet a lot of people, go a lot of places, get a lot of invitations, because you can play golf well. Use your golf that way and you'll find it'll be much more fun."

I took his advice but I have never seen him again. I came close in 1980 when I was scheduled to play in a PGA Seniors Pro-Am in Florida. I registered for the single reason his name was on the list. If nothing else, I wanted to shake his hand and tell him I'd taken his advice. When I arrived, I found out he couldn't make it. I was really disappointed because it would have been a high point in my life to play in a tournament with him. Down inside I suspect he would never have remembered me, but I wanted to see him. He was my hero and I wish Mr. Sarazen had been there.

For a teenager to have officer friends was a real privilege. Lieutenant Calhoun, a pilot at Nichols Field, became a good friend. Occasionally he'd call and I'd get to fly with him in a little observation airplane. He had to fly a certain amount to get in his navigational requirements and was generous to think of the kid who could play golf and wanted to be a pursuit pilot. On several occasions we flew up to Baguio (a beautiful mountain resort area), landed, pulled out our golf sticks, played a round of golf, then flew back to Manila. It was fantastic for me, playing golf and unknowingly getting insight into the very thing I hoped would be my life's work.

At sixteen I managed to find out that young hormones can really get out of control. Paula, a lieutenant's wife, took a shine to me. She was a beautiful girl—swimmer, badminton player, golfer, and had the figure to make her look professional at almost anything. I guess her interest began on the badminton court. As I recall, I was post champion at the time, and since she played a lot of badminton, I saw her very often at the club and the pool. One thing led to another and eventually she had the dubious honor of deflowering me. No doubt more people knew about it than I ever imagined. One evening, my father brought up the subject of Paula and pointed out the potential dangers of such a relationship. Being a little embarrassed and not knowing really what to say, I reeled off some profound statement about how much fun it was. One of the few outbursts I can remember from my father followed, and I learned in a hurry and beyond any reasonable doubt, this was no laughing matter. He didn't know it, but two days before, I leaped over a second-story railing and fell into some kind of tropical bush while making a very hasty exit from her bedroom in total panic. I told Dad very truthfully that it was over, and it was.

When Kay came along, it was a whole new ballgame. She

was pretty, athletic, and as nice a person as you could want to meet. Before long we were going steady, though she was only fifteen and I was seventeen. Her father had started her playing golf and she took to it like the accomplished athlete she was. She won the post ladies' championship, shooting a consistent 76 to 82. Since we both lived on post, we went everywhere together and our relationship remained serious for a long time.

General Douglas MacArthur didn't help me any, but maybe he was working a different problem. In 1935, MacArthur came over and set up his home and headquarters in the Manila Hotel. Major Dwight Eisenhower was his chief of staff, as MacArthur had been brought back to serve the Army by reconstituting the Philippine Army. He later chose other people to serve on his staff, including my father to advise on medical matters. As a result, we moved from Fort McKinley to Perez Street in downtown Manila, near the old Tabacalera cigar factory, in the summer of 1937. That kind of complicated my relationship with Kay, though it didn't stop it. I simply hitchhiked about ten miles back to Fort McKinley to see her when I could. However, my immaturity and complications resulting from moving Army families saw to it that our lives took different directions. Ultimately she married a fighter pilot who rose to the rank of major general in the Air Force, but it was not my privilege to see her from the day she got married in 1942 until March 1967, when I was ferrying an F-4 from the States to Vietnam.

CHAPTER 3

West Point

It was Friday, 17 December 1943—one of the most important days of my life and I knew it. At 4:00 P.M. (1600 hours military time), all the cadets would go to appointed sally ports, as they did every Friday, and read the results of the week's academic effort. But this was a special week, at least for those of us who had requested pilot training. We had been told when we signed up early in the spring that flight training would be provided only to those cadets who were proficient in all subjects at Christmas 1943. Then, if selected, training would begin 1 April 1944 at specified airfields in the south and southwest.

I was not an outstanding student. I never really learned how to study until 1939 when I got to the West Point prep school in San Francisco—Drews Preparatory School. In high school I skipped class a lot, wrote many notes explaining my absence, and, in general, was just too satisfied with mediocre-to-poor performance. I never failed anything but I came dangerously close a few times. At Drews, I began to learn the meaning of "stick-to-it." At year's end I passed the mental exam to West Point but was shocked to learn I had failed the physical. It seemed I had a spot on my chest X ray "in the left hylar region," and was disqualified. That led me to the University of

Denver, my cousin Lila Lee, and, at the end of the first year, a job in a molybdenum mine in Climax, Colorado.

About halfway through the summer of 1941, my father called to tell me the regulation had been changed and asked if I still wanted to go to the Academy. That answer was easy—I had never gotten over that emptiness I felt when I realized I could not go to West Point. I never really considered anything else. Wanting to go to West Point went back a long way. I started at age eight, watching cadets come home on Christmas leave.

In the Philippines there was a river I had to cross when I rode the trolley from Fort McKinley back to Manila. It took about ten seconds to go across that river on the trolley, and somehow I believed if I could get a prayer out in that time, it would come true. It was always the same—"Please, God, let me go to West Point and let me become a great fighter pilot." Time after time, I pleaded for my life to take that direction. Oh, yes, I still wanted to go to West Point!

Four days after leaving Colorado I arrived in Washington, D.C., where I immediately enrolled in Millards Prep School. We went through the appropriate books seven times between August 1941 and the end of November. It was study, study, study. We took examinations each Saturday morning, and in the afternoon I would get dressed up and troop the halls of Congress explaining to any congressman who would listen why I wanted to go to West Point. I needed a congressional appointment—some representatives appointed outright, others selected their appointee by giving competitive Civil Service exams. One Saturday afternoon I visited the office of Congressman Sullivan from Missouri. He'd never had a graduate from his five appointees and had, just moments before, dictated a letter announcing his new procedure to hold a competitive exam for his appointment. Mr. Sullivan told me I could take his exam and if I won it I would get the spot. I took the exam in November 1941 and was waiting for the results when Pearl Harbor was attacked. I was notified on 18 December I had won the appointment and was ordered by the War Department to report to the U.S. Military Academy at West Point on 1 July 1942.

So getting to West Point was not easy, but my first year of academics was deceptive. We had many subjects I already had either in high school or during my year at the University of Denver. I guess at the end of the first half year at West Point (Christmas 1942), I was in the top twenty percent of the class. Then it happened—new and harder subjects—some of which I had no background in whatsoever. I began sliding dramatically and by early October 1943 it was obvious I was in trouble.

I had to study after taps (10:00 P.M.), so each night I went to the basement shower room armed with a flashlight and a blanket. One of the upperclassmen was helping me, but every week it was nip and tuck. Calculus, chemistry, and economics seemed to occupy ninety percent of my time, and each week I would be proficient in two and down in one. Week after week—up two, down one—the names changed but the result was the same. Finally it was Friday, 17 December 1943, and in a few minutes I was going to walk across the "area" to the sally port and see which direction my life was going. To fly was as much a part of my ambition as going to the Academy, so I felt I just had to be accepted for pilot training. Life as a ground cadet the rest of my time at West Point and tons of paperwork and wasted time awaited me if I was not proficient in all subjects that day.

My legs were so weak I stumbled leaving the building. Crossing the area to the sally port, my heart was pounding so hard I could feel my face flush. The grades were posted in three or four different places, so I searched frantically for the classes I was in. There was the first of the three troublemakers, 2.1. Not good but passing. My eyes raced down the long sheet of cadet names and grades. There's the second one, 2.1 again. Only one to go, and not since early September had I been proficient in all three the same week. I couldn't find the third one—back over the list again with my heart pounding so I could hardly see. It means so much, please, God, don't forget the fighter-pilot part of my prayer. There it was finally, 2.0! They must have felt sorry for me, but who cares. I made it! Air Cadet Blesse strode out of the sally port weak-kneed and misty-eyed with thanks. Frank Lish, my roommate, called over to me, "You make it okay?"

"Of course," I replied, my voice cracking slightly, "was there any doubt?"

It seemed like years later, but 1 April 1944 finally arrived and I found myself heading for Pine Bluff, Arkansas, for primary flight training. Physical training, ground school, and flying would now occupy ninety-eight percent of my time until primary was complete. Physical training was fun, ground school was interesting, and the flying seemed too good to be true.

My instructor was a short, rather rotund little gentleman named Floyd V. Pengra. He was demanding enough to make us learn, but he always seemed to remember that we had to love flying if we were going to be good. He absorbed the dumb things we did, kicked us in the fanny to set us straight, then went right on instructing as though nothing had happened. He was great.

Three weeks after arrival at Pine Bluff I was "bouncing" in the pattern, and after four landings Mr. Pengra told me to taxi in. I taxied the little PT-19 back near our operations tent and Mr. Pengra got out of the backseat and yelled in my ear, "This is too dangerous for me. You go fly by yourself, and be careful. There is a large mud hole at the far end of the field." After five or six hours' dual instruction, it never occurred to me I couldn't do it, so I lined up for takeoff and launched myself into an aviation career that lasted thirty years. Did everything go smoothly on my first solo flight? Of course not. After shooting several landings, I taxied into the hole Mr. Pengra had warned me about. I was "Mud Hole Blesse" for several weeks.

Dad had gone to North Africa as surgeon general for the theater commander, General Eisenhower, so I delighted in writing him all the new things that were happening to me.

The summer sped by. Flying was all I had hoped it would be, and to make things even better, I met a very lovely young lady in Pine Bluff. Joe had dark hair, beautiful dark eyes, and a marvelous figure. Before long, we were going as steady as time would permit. By the time my training at Pine Bluff was complete, we were thinking of more permanent things and continued to do so through the fall and winter of 1944. However, as graduation, more flying, and combat loomed in the immediate future, I really felt I wasn't ready to get married and that wonderful relationship came to a close. Joe was a beautiful, stable, well-educated young lady and deserved better treatment than I felt I was going to be able to provide her.

After a couple of months of primary training in the PT-19, we all headed back to New York to take basic training in the AT-6. All the remaining training we got was done at Stewart Field, eighteen miles north of West Point. "Basic" was relatively uneventful except I got busted for taking an aircraft without the instructor's permission. The operations sergeant said he had an extra aircraft and asked if I wanted to fly. "Why not," I said, and spent several months walking the area with a nine-pound Garand rifle over my shoulder as a result of that hasty decision.

Academics dragged through the summer and fall of 1944, into the gloom period after Christmas, but finally it was spring. We were off to Stewart Field full-time to take advanced training. We learned to fly at night and had hour after hour of instrument practice. April and May of 1945 passed quickly, and before I knew it the plans for getting our wings and graduation from West Point were being laid before us.

During Advanced I had a strange experience. We were at an auxiliary field for night flying—two shifts, and I was on the last one. When I reported to fly, the instructor was already in the backseat since he had just flown with another cadet. I was expected to make an inspection of the aircraft before I got in, so I began my usual walkaround, which included engine and prop inspection.

There was a lot of noise and confusion in the darkness since we were parked almost wingtip to wingtip, and some aircraft were already taxiing out to fly. As I continued my inspection, I came down the wing under the cowl and then froze as though I didn't know where to go next. The engine and prop were ahead of me; I knew that very well. My mind seemed to go blank as I stood there under the cowl, and I did absolutely nothing for at least fifteen seconds. About that time the instructor reduced throttle, the engine backfired, and for the first time it dawned on me the engine was running. Had I taken two more steps to inspect the engine and prop I would have been cut to pieces.

To this day, I don't know why I stopped under that cowling. Something turned me off mentally and I simply couldn't move. I can only assume the Lord felt He had other things for me to do. It wasn't time yet, and though I didn't understand it, I was very thankful. After all, I had a brother-in-law who had been shot down in a B-17 and was a prisoner in Germany. I had another brother-in-law who was taken prisoner at Corregidor in the Philippines, and my father had been in North Africa and Italy for over two years. It was my time to join the war effort and I had thought of nothing else for the last year. I couldn't wait.

My dad, stepmother, and sister all attended my graduation along with Congressman Sullivan of Missouri. He reminded me I was his first appointee to graduate, and I was delighted he took time to attend. Dad pinned my Air Corps wings on me, and upon graduation on 5 June 1945, I felt maybe I had repaid him for all the anxiety and trouble that seem to be part of raising a son.

CHAPTER 4

The Real World

Before reporting for my first duty station, I had a month's leave, so I headed back to Washington, D.C. It was quite an experience coming home from West Point in an Army Air Force uniform complete with second lieutenant's bars and pilot's wings. Dad was still in Washington and the old house he bought in 1941 out in Spring Valley looked just the same. After I'd been there a week, I told Dad I'd like to go out and bum around the country before reporting for duty and see what's changed. I had been a happy hermit since 1942.

The B-4 bag was quickly packed and Dad dropped me off at Bolling Field. I caught the first westbound B-25, changed planes twice, and finally made it to Stapleton Field in Denver where I hotfooted it over to see Lila Lee. We had always been close as kids, but during my year in Denver we got much closer and kind of grew up together. While I stayed on base and she was at home, we saw each other every night, renewing old times, doing all the things we used to do—dancing at Lakeside to the big bands and thoroughly enjoying each other's company. If she hadn't been my cousin, I'm sure I would have married her. They don't come any nicer.

After about a week, I went down to Texas, played in a golf tournament, and then headed back east. In Washington, D.C., I bought a '41 Ford V-8 convertible and began getting ready for

my first assignment—P-40 training at Napier Field in Dothan,
Alabama. I reported 1 July 1945.

The P-40 was outclassed early in the war, but everybody,
especially me, thought flying it was a big deal. This was the
fighter the Flying Tigers had made famous with its grinning
shark's teeth, and it had a glamorous aura of combat that gave
us new shavetails a lift to be flying it. Since the war in Europe
had ended just before I graduated, all of us were looking forward to getting into combat in the Pacific as soon as possible.

Checking out in a new aircraft in 1945 was vastly different
from the way it is done now. They gave us a manual, which we
studied briefly, then we went out and flew. They figured you
had wings and this was just another airplane. During July we
learned to fly the P-40 in a very limited way. When our training
was completed, I only had about ten or eleven hours in type,
but it was a lot of fun and a fine teacher for the Mustang, which
was supposed to be next. We were scheduled for a P-51 RTU
(replacement training unit), but lo and behold, they sent us to
Orlando, Florida, for a month at Junior Staff Officers School!
No one wanted to fly a desk, but there was no arguing, so we
went to administrative school in August 1945. The shooting
ended 2 September, and so did our hopes of becoming a part of
the "Big War."

No one knew what to do with us. We were new warriors
without a war. Finally an assignment came through to Dale
Mabry Field, Florida, for the long-awaited P-51 training. What
I remember vividly is the degradation of the Army Air Forces
at that base. My first visit to the officers' club was an eye-
opener; there was a stripper performing who left nothing to
your imagination except maybe wondering if she were double-
jointed in some unusual spots. Maybe I was just a little too
naive or hadn't seen enough war, but this display didn't im-
press me at all. I liked girls, enjoyed their company, being with
them, and I enjoyed the chase and the catch, but to watch
them prance around the floor and flaunt it at you didn't do
much for me.

Before we got checked out in the P-51, word arrived that Dale Mabry Air Base was going to be closed, so we were sent back to Dothan. But they didn't know what to do with us, either. By this time, there were about fifty thousand people milling around aimlessly, waiting to be processed out of the service. Our small Regular Army bunch of fifty-two didn't fit into any of the AAF's plans. "We don't know what to do with you guys, but we'll get around to you when we get all these other people processed." Our first lesson in "hurry up and wait."

After we hung around Dothan until it became obvious they really didn't have anything for us, we all got jobs. I worked as an assistant to an electrician in town. We had guys working for the state as surveyor's helpers, others doing odd jobs, all of us second lieutenants in the Army Air Force. By October, I got pretty tired of it and told my roommates, "I'm going to Washington—give me a call if anything happens." We had been informed there would be two or three days' warning if we got assignments.

I drove up to Washington, D.C., and everyone was glad to see me. Dad asked how everything was going, but when he found out I was there without orders he really got nervous. After spending all his life in the service, as far as he was concerned, I was AWOL and in for a court-martial. About ten or twelve days later, I got a call from my buddies to get back for a big meeting Monday morning. I drove back, made the meeting, and off we went to Hunter Field, Georgia. There was nothing to do there either. There weren't even any airplanes to fly since all they were doing was delivering P-51s to some boneyard. That sounded better than nothing, but when we tried to get in on some ferry flying, we were told if we hadn't been, we couldn't go. It was as simple as that, so they gave us odd jobs not involving flying.

I did manage to get checked out in the P-51 at Hunter Field. I was airdrome officer one Friday, and a young major with a fifty-mission crush to his hat taxied a P-51 up to be parked. I got him all the information he needed, then gave him a ride into Base Ops. He would be there three days. Before he left, almost in a joking manner, I mentioned flying his P-51. He said that would be okay but be sure it was refueled and ready to go Sunday by about 4:00 P.M. I thought he ought to know I had never flown one before, but he replied there was a manual in the map carrier in the cockpit.

That weekend I put about five hours on the major's aircraft and had it ready for him on Sunday. I would have felt different about missing WW II that day if I had known that in five years I'd be flying a Mustang in Korea.

Not long after we arrived at Hunter AFB, they put me in charge of a work group consisting of twenty-five prisoners. I was informed it was in the mill to give the base back to the city and the Army wanted to know how much drainage pipe had been put in so they could charge the city accordingly. After a small demonstration of what they wanted, I was given the task of locating and recording the locations of all the drainage pipe on the airfield, its diameter, and all associated information. I was still classifying pipe when fifty-two of us got hush-hush orders on 20 December 1945 to report to Salt Lake City. No Christmas leave, just get there and keep your mouth shut. It was hush-hush all right—Salt Lake City didn't know why we were there, either, so we entered limbo status again.

Though I don't remember doing much at Salt Lake, I did get in a little flying. One guy was current in the L-5, a little liaison airplane. The airbase had several with no one to fly them, so the pilot who was checked out got several of us qualified. For a week we flew them in twos, having a great time dogfighting and doing a lot of things we probably shouldn't have been doing. At least we learned to fly a new airplane.

After about a month another set of orders came through—we were to go to Nichols Field in the Philippines via ship! We left in late January 1946. It was a typical troopship—everything was seven pounds in a four-pound bag. When we arrived in the Philippines, it was the same old thing again. They didn't have anything for us to do, so they put us in big twelve-man tents. It was miserable. Rats all over the damned place with everyone sleeping under mosquito nets, not because of mosquitoes but to prevent the rats from running all over us. Several times at night, I was brought bolt upright in my sack when some character decided to blast a rat off of a nearby shelf. After that happened a few times, sensible heads prevailed and that became prohibited. No firing allowed at snakes or rats. Although we stayed there about a month, I don't remember doing anything constructive.

Finally more orders arrived. Our group of fifty-two was split into three parts—one-third went to Japan to fly P-51s, a third went to a P-47 group on Okinawa, and the remainder stayed in the Philippines to be assigned to Florida Blanca Air Base. I drew Okinawa.

Before I left for Okinawa, I made it a point to get to Fort McKinley (where I used to live), to Stotsenberg, Clark Field, Baguio, and all the places that had meant so much to me just a few years before. It seemed impossible only five years had elapsed, as everything was in a state of ruin. The Japanese had not maintained the golf course at McKinley, so it was overgrown and actually ruined. The old gym where we played basketball on Saturday mornings was still in good shape, but few buildings remained untouched by the war. The memories flowed like computer data as I drove from one end of the post to the other. It was depressing to see my old house, right across the street from the fourth green. There was literally nothing left—it was burned to the ground. The cement steps in front were untouched but the house itself had undoubtedly taken a direct bomb hit. Only five years ago I was a kid playing golf, going to school, hoping to go to West Point, wanting to fly, and now, in a snap of the fingers, I was back a lieutenant in the Air Corps almost wondering how it all happened.

CHAPTER 5

Island Living

We arrived on Okinawa in early March 1946 and were assigned to the 1st Squadron of the 413th Fighter Group based at Yontan. The field was on the western side of the island about midway from a north/south viewpoint.

The squadron area was arranged with several long plywood buildings in the same general area, each comprised of two main rooms. There were showers and toilets in a conveniently located building, with other buildings erected by the pilots for special interests like photography, ice-cream making, and the like. We had one or two handball courts and an open-air movie theater.

Our quarters were like a small two-bedroom apartment with a central room and two bedrooms off of it. Closets were large and, in general, the accommodations were quite good considering where we were. My roommate was named John Noble, an accomplished pianist. Jesse Hearin, Ray Jones, Bob Eckert, Bob Valpy, and one or two other classmates were all in the 1st Squadron with me. All in all it wasn't too bad.

Looking around the island was dangerous, since a few Japanese holdouts still remained. All caves were off-limits, and the presence of mines had to be considered wherever you went. Not one building was standing on Okinawa when I arrived in March 1946. The roads were two-lane coral with few markings to tell you where they led, so initially we didn't stray too far from Yontan Air Base.

The name of the game was to make life as easy as possible, and there was war-surplus stuff all over the island. Initially, abandoned equipment was everywhere, but as Okinawa came back to life, the leavings were gathered up and stored in an area about a mile square. During the war, if a guy was driving a jeep and anything went wrong, it was pushed off to the side of the road and he got another vehicle. If the mechanics couldn't find the problem fast, the vehicle went to the scrapyard.

We made regular expeditions to the scrapyard, picking up anything we even thought might be of use. We found a jeep that had only a bad fuel pump and repaired it. Then came a motorcycle, which I bought for ten dollars when Gus Breen went home on emergency leave. It wasn't running but we had plenty of time to fix it. We also found a forty-two-foot liberty boat. Captain Willie Walker was the maintenance magician among us; he could fix anything in the world. Jesse, Oscar, and the rest of us with weak minds and strong bodies did Willie's bidding. We stripped the top off this boat and built a new cabin, cleaned off the paint, recaulked it, then put it back together and painted it. For a case of whiskey on the Navy side we got two brand-new Gray marine diesel engines still in the crates. We had parties on that boat, fished from it, and had tremendous fun with it for about a year and a half. We eventually sold it when our two years were up and it was time to return home.

Willie had sent to the States for a 1938 or 1939 four-door Chevy. He really fixed that thing up, using it for dates; everyone had a terrific time. We had the deal on transportation sewed up until the island got more sophisticated and the MPs set up roadblocks, trying to get back all the government equipment. If you didn't have a trip ticket, they'd take the vehicle away. One of our friends in the motor pool gave us a book of blank tickets, so every morning we'd make out a trip ticket and go wherever we wanted.

We would never have been caught, but during a P-47 deployment to Japan we loaned the jeep while we were gone. The borrower forgot to fill out a ticket one day and they picked up our jeep. We still had the Chevy and the motorcycle, but we mourned the loss of that jeep.

We thought putting a sidecar on the cycle would make it safer, but the guys kept having accidents with it, anyway. On one of our trips to procure gas inside a barbed-wire compound, who should we run into but Gus Breen, who had unexpectedly come back from his leave. He was there with a Red Cross girl in a truck and, showing off just a wee bit, he asked if he could ride the cycle he had sold me. I said yes, but it had a sidecar now. "Oh, hell," said Gus, "I've ridden these things all my life."

"Yeah, maybe," I replied, "but never with a sidecar—it's entirely different." Off he went without listening.

Ole Gus started off, roaring from one end of the compound to the other. There was a hole, about five feet wide and two feet deep, just before one corner. It had been raining so all you could see was a smooth puddle of water. Gus came tearing down there and we could see him leaning, expecting the cycle to turn. Of course, it didn't turn at all. Before we knew it, he had overshot the turn and the front wheel went down into the hole. The back end came over his shoulder and threw him against the fence. The cycle bounced off but Gus's feet got caught on the barbed wire, hanging him about five feet from the ground, head down. He was being such a smart-ass that it seemed fitting it should happen to him. All of us, including the Red Cross girl, were laughing so hard we could barely function as we tried to help him. We finally got him off the fence but he was all cut up.

In spite of our many accidents with the cycle, Jesse kept wanting a crack at checking out. When we got the sidecar, it looked like the time was ripe. Our living area was a semicircle with the main road closing the two ends, so I had him drive around in the semicircle with me in the sidecar. A convoy was going by and right across one of the open legs was the chaplain's house. We were zipping around the circle, and as we got closer to the main road there was a helluva lot of these trucks going by about thirty or forty feet apart. Jesse got confused and turned the throttle the wrong way—he was going to stop and let the convoy go by, but he shot right at one of them. Fortunately it went by and we kind of hit the space between that truck and the next one coming, shooting directly across the road and onto the front stairs of the chaplain's quarters.

The front wheel hit the front door and flattened it. The chaplain was inside reading and damn near had a heart attack—the cycle was roaring away at full throttle, trying to get into the living room, but the sidecar had it stuck in the doorjamb, bucking back and forth. I'm trying to get Jesse to shut the engine off all this time and we finally sat there and laughed like hell. I'm sure to this day, the chaplain thought we were crazy. Well, anyway, Jesse was now checked out.

Another time a guy got drunk over at one of the club parties and, without saying anything, took the cycle. He ended up driving it down an embankment, into a thicket—it took us two hours to get the cycle out. If he hadn't come back in the club all cut up, we would never have found it.

After about the seventh accident, the squadron commander demanded we get rid of the thing, so we took it to the other side of the island and sold it for $100. Too bad, particularly since all the other vehicles except Willie's Chevy had been confiscated by then.

When I got to Okinawa in early 1946, there were only two or three American girls. We hardly ever saw any gals since most worked in administrative units on the other side of the island. They were Red Cross and Army girls at first, but by the time we'd been there six or seven months, their number had multiplied considerably and little night clubs started springing up everywhere. A unit would find a Quonset hut, scrounge the building materials, and literally build a club with dance floor, small stage, and bar. The overall theme was usually tropical, all decked out with appropriate plants just like downtown. After a year on Okinawa, there were some really nice places to go and some very nice girls to go with you.

When Willie Walker got married in 1947, I was his best man. The bride's maid of honor was a girl named Dorothy. Dotty was really a nice girl and very attractive, but not very outgoing with me. I guess her Army boyfriend saw to that. Toward the end of my tour on Okinawa she took a boat trip to the Philippines, so I flew down fifteen days later to meet the boat. We visited a few of my old stomping grounds: shopping, swimming, and the Army-Navy Club in the evening. She went back to Long Beach and that was that, but our paths would cross again.

The pilots were all happy-go-lucky on the ground, and we got to know each other all too well. Don Stuck had an unusual fetish: he was a nut about getting fat or overeating, so naturally he was as thin as a rail. We decided to break him of telling us we shouldn't eat pies, ice cream, cookies, and other goodies, so one night while he was sleeping, we got his webbed uniform belt off his trousers and shaved about $\frac{1}{16}$th inch off it. We replaced the buckle and put the belt back on his pants.

There was no immediate result, but after about three nights of shaving a tiny bit off, we noticed Don was not eating some portions of his meals. We continued to shave his belt and he continued to reduce his intake of food, being thoroughly convinced he was gaining weight. We got him down about six pounds before he caught us shaving his belt. He was furious! But he never mentioned desserts or diets or overweight problems again.

We didn't do much when we first got to Okinawa—there were only two or three airplanes in commission. The pilots knew they were going home, and they were just waiting to be transferred. Flying had virtually stopped on the island; no training, nothing. Since we were the first people to arrive after the war, they decided to check us out in the P-47, so finally, nine months after graduation, life as a fighter pilot began. As it turned out it wasn't all that great. In fact, I can remember writing my dad commenting that it was a rather "harem, scarem existence."

The first ten or fifteen hours in the P-47 were exciting, to say the least. The aircraft had been put in temporary storage when the war ended, so rubber hoses, fuel lines, and the like had deteriorated over the past seven or eight months.

On one of those early flights I experienced complete engine failure and had to get back to our little 4,000-foot coral strip at Yontan. Yontan was in the central part of the island where it narrowed on the west coast. The strip looked short, with a big coral pit on the south end waiting to swallow me up, but I got down with no further trouble. Later, on another flight, I was drenched with 100-octane gas when I rolled the aircraft on its back. I don't know why the thing didn't blow up. When I rolled it back over, gas was swishing back and forth along the rudder-pedal runners. I eased the throttle back delicately and headed for home. Entering the traffic pattern, I was as smooth as I could be and set it down on the runway like a butterfly with sore feet—half waiting for the backfire that would turn me into a torch. I braked gently to a stop, cut the engine, climbed overboard, and started running. It never did burn but I don't know why.

Being inexperienced those first hours in the Thunderbolt, I hadn't been briefed or didn't remember what the P-47 did when put into a steep dive. To recover, you needed to add power. If you pulled the throttle back, the dive angle steepened. I got into that situation during one of my first dive-bombing runs. I rolled into a steep dive that looked like it was about 60°. Picking up speed, I began a pullout with little success. I instinctively cut the throttle back and the nose tucked under, steepening my dive. Then I got both hands on the stick and pulled as hard as I could. I was sitting there hauling on the stick with all my might. I actually lost sight of the water and everything else, because by pulling so many Gs, I slid down in the seat below the canopy sill. I couldn't have missed the water by much more than 100 feet; zooming back into the sky, I finally got slow enough to regain control. No one ever had to brief me on that again!

There was a little island called Tonaki Shima west of Okinawa that had some old Japanese barges left on the beach. They were great bombing and strafing targets. When I had about ten hours in the P-47, a guy named Sanger and I flew over and dropped our bombs, then strafed the barges. About the third pass, pulling off the target, my engine quit and the big four-bladed prop began windmilling, acting like a huge air brake. I switched tanks and did everything I could think of, but couldn't get any power. I chandelled up to about 2,500 feet, radioed Sanger, told him the engine quit, and said I was getting out. That was all I had time for. The Thunderbolt glides like a sewer cover and we had all been warned not to try to belly it into the water. That much I remembered.

As I rolled back the electrically actuated canopy, I could see I was losing altitude rapidly. Around 1,300 or 1,400 feet, I tried to go over the side but I had failed to detach my oxygen hose. If it had been anything else, I would have felt the pull immediately, but that rubber hose stretched out like an accordion. I got myself half over the side, about ready to jump, and this damned oxygen hose was like an umbilical cord. I climbed back in, pulled it loose from the base, and went over the side as quickly as I could. By this time I was really low. I pulled the ripcord and then three things happened so rapidly I never knew the sequence—the jerk of the chute opening, explosion of the '47 hitting the water, and fighting from about twenty feet underwater to get to the surface. Later I was told by a fisherman a half mile away that he thought I hit the water before my parachute opened. I don't doubt it looked that way—the chute barely opened and I was descending too fast when I hit the water. I wasn't bruised, but I did go a long way under before popping to the surface.

Suddenly I found myself treading water in the third most shark-infested body of water in the world. Pulling my shoes off helped a little; then I tried my one-man life raft. Off came the clips, zipper opened, and I laid it out on the water and pulled the lanyard the way we had been told. Nothing happened. In the meantime, I hadn't been smart enough to inflate my Mae West; too much excitement, I guess. I was treading water all this time and it never occurred to me I had a life preserver on—I was just going to get in that rubber boat. I was getting tired as hell.

I laid that raft out in the water a few more times and pulled the lanyard like I thought I was supposed to. Treading water, I held this damn thing up in the air off the water and read the instructions on it—sure enough, it said pull the lanyard twice, so I pulled it twice more and nothing happened. By now I wasn't tired, I was *tired!* It finally dawned on me I had a Mae West. I mean, they don't put gold bars on cadets for nothing. I pulled the lanyard on the left—nothing. Pulled on the right—it puffed right up. Thank God! Then, just like I was told, I unscrewed the little valve on the left side, which wouldn't work automatically, and blew into it until it was inflated.

Wasting no time, I went back to working on that little raft. No matter what I did, I couldn't get it to inflate, so I reluctantly decided to let it go. I poked my head underwater to watch it go down three, four, five, six feet until it finally disappeared. With the area's reputation for sharks, I couldn't help thinking I was watching my best chance for survival sink to the bottom.

Fortunately, the fisherman who saw me go down came over and fished me out. After considerable thrashing around, I finally fell exhausted in the back of his boat. Sanger had called back to base, so in about twenty minutes or so an SA-16 Grumman amphibian landed in the water, took me aboard, and flew me back to Yontan.

I was young and inexperienced, so all the old heads had a ball with the intelligence debriefing. They were full of all kinds of questions. I told them the damn raft just didn't work, the cylinder was bad. More questions—it was beginning to sound as though I was on trial. I was glad I had stretched the raft out in the water and read the instructions, because when I told them that the inquisition stopped. They were finally satisfied the equipment just did not work.

Though the Thunderbolts were marginal, eventually we got in a lot of flying and training. My flight commander, Don Stuck, was a great pilot. He later went to work as a test pilot for McDonnell Douglas. Our most frequent mission was a four-ship flight for navigation and tactics. Usually there was a flight leader, an experienced element leader, and two of us inexperienced types. The leader would let us lead for a while, navigate from this place to that place, then he'd take over again for some tactics. He would put us in trail, doing rolls and loops while following the leader. Finally we'd split up in two-plane elements, get in trail again, and this time, instead of doing everything smooth and easy, we would "rat-race." The leaders would really start moving the airplane around to see if they could shake us off. They didn't try very hard for a while, but as we started getting better they had to work harder to lose us. We were learning.

It was an excellent training for us neophytes, and we absorbed a great deal, but we lost a couple of guys. Once in a while the leader or wingman would misjudge while plunging through a damn cloud. If it was just a small cloud, you could go in and out of it before anything happened, but in a large one, it was easy to lose control and end up in a spin before coming out the other side. None of us were very good at instrument flying; we never flew the '47s at night, but used AT-6s instead. Believe me, inside a cloud, inverted, it was easy to get excited and end up spinning out the bottom into the water. We lost a couple that way.

We lost a few pilots buzzing, too, including Roger Ramey. Ward Protsman got so low once he bent his prop blades back 90° at the tips, but he made it back okay.

There were other losses. One was my roommate, John Noble, who could really play the piano. I had always wanted to learn, but I was a little too flighty to sit down and practice every day, so John said he would teach me. He started off with the basics but soon realized I was getting bored. "Tell you what, Boots, I'll teach you a few bars of boogie woogie and whenever you get frustrated you can bang away, realizing that you'll eventually get better and things will be all right." In a couple of weeks, I could sit down and whack out about a minute of boogie that'd make you think I was a real piano player. Problem was, as soon as I ran out of the memorized part, I was through and had to find some way to get off or admit that's all I knew. Anyway, we went on with the lessons.

A short time later, John got in a dogfight with a P-61 night fighter, which could turn pretty tight—the P-47N didn't turn all that well. The Jug and that Black Widow really got to hacking it around and John spun in, killing himself. It's a sad reminder that to this day that's all the piano playing I can do—about 30 or 40 seconds of boogie woogie—then I get up and say, "Well, hell, I'm not in the mood."

When ships came in from the States, it was always a big event, so we'd fly out ten or fifteen miles and meet them. Right on the water we would pull up, roll over the ship, and put on an air show for them. I'm surprised we never killed anybody doing that, since we flew those Jugs on the edge all the time, trying to dream up some form of fun.

We lost one or two pilots testing aircraft after routine maintenance work. We lost Jack Ray, a guy from Hastings, Nebraska, during an engine test hop. When a new or overhauled engine was installed, we were told to "slow time" it for a few hours to break it in. The idea was to take off at less than full power—actually, with as little power as possible to get it off and fly it around. It was a stupid idea; I don't know where it ever started. Jack took off and continued down the runway with too little power until right near the end of the runway, when he realized he wasn't going to make it. He started to feed in throttle but it was too late. He clipped the landing gear on something, skidded back into the ground, and flipped inverted into a rice paddy. As I recall, he wasn't killed in the crash, but he drowned in the shallow water when the aircraft flipped over and trapped him underneath. He was a hell of a good guy; we used to refer to him as Jack Armstrong with his ruddy complexion and good looks.

On Okinawa, because of the humidity, we found most days you could pull vapor streamers off your wingtips if you pulled tight enough on the break—the initial turn over the runway for landing. This led to a "talent" we young pilots attempted to acquire—minimum-time traffic patterns. One of the most beautiful sights you'll ever see is a fighter peeling up off the deck, trailing streamers off the wingtips in a tight-turning traffic pattern. We had a combat veteran named Wagner who could occasionally hit 29 seconds in the P-47N from peelup to touchdown. Don Stuck was another master of the pattern; he could make it in 30 to 32 seconds all the time. Frankly, it was a good way to bust your ass—and many guys did—if you didn't learn it in stages. It was like any other fighter-pilot technique, though—some could do it and others could tell you why it was such a dumb idea. An F-86 made a beautiful pattern but I never got it below 35 seconds in my life, and even that seemed like it was too tight for comfort. As the aircraft got faster, the radius of turn increased and it just plain took longer to make the circle. You'll never see anything like that today because the safety implications are such that it just isn't worth the risk. Twenty-four out of twenty-five may be good skeet shooting, but it's a career buster for a wing commander.

Every day we had a group effort called a Scooter Alert. Two P-47s were always loaded with live ammunition, sitting on alert, but they usually didn't scramble except on Saturdays and Sundays when we weren't working. The Sunday morning Scooter Alert was fun because we'd go north out over the water very early in the morning and scream in on the deck, 20 to 30 feet above the trees, flying the whole length of the island and waking everyone up. It was a lot of fun, but like many of the other things we routinely did soon after the war, we had to stop it. Very gradually the process of professionalism was setting in. Fewer pilots were being killed needlessly but the pure fun of "harem, scarem" flying was disappearing.

Around mid-March 1946, General Ennis Whitehead came down from 5th Air Force in Japan on an inspection trip. Upon seeing the degradation he began ripping rear ends, starting with the group commander. In no uncertain terms, he told our CO that things were going to change. He wanted a fifty-ship flyby before the end of May, which gave two months to get the group back in operation. The resulting big stir caused flying to begin in earnest and Okinawa came back to life.

On 19 May we had the flyby. There were seventeen aborts that afternoon and I was one of them. On takeoff, climbing out over the water, an oil line broke, throwing hot black oil all over the windshield, me, and everything else. To see at all I had to crack the canopy open about a foot, then I headed back. I sideslipped that P-47 down the final approach like I had a forty-knot crosswind; it was the only way I could see to land. There was also a midair collision that afternoon when two guys ran into each other in formation and had to bail out. It was a real fiasco, but about what you'd expect after so much inactivity followed by a hard push to perform. Not only was the equipment in questionable shape but the pilots and leaders were a bit rusty as well.

Starting about May 1946, reassignments began rolling in for the vets to return Stateside. We began losing people and soon there weren't enough airmen to maintain the aircraft. By the end of June, we had maybe six airmen in the squadron. Two of them were in the orderly room, one was a cook, and that left three to manage the flight line. The most experienced man was made line chief and a couple of staff sergeants became flight chiefs.

The squadron commander got the pilots together and passed on the news that if we wanted to fly, we'd have to maintain our own planes. "After you get the work done, go to the flight chief and then the line chief to get it inspected." Those of us who chose to do so worked like that from the latter part of June through October, when we started getting people back in the squadron again. Reviewing my Form Five (flying-time record) for that period, I see I flew a very cautious ten or twelve hours a month, never out of sight of the base! That was an interesting experiment to say the least, but we seemed to survive; in fact, we enjoyed it.

Looking back on that first year on Okinawa, we lost a lot of guys due to airplanes in lousy shape, poor maintenance, and pilot error. By the time I left, out of nineteen pilots all but three or four had bailed out at least once, several jumped twice, and one man three times. The last time for that lucky pilot he was climbing through 17,000 and the '47 just blew up—he found himself flying in his parachute. When he got back to the field he said, "That's it! I've had enough of these fighters. I'm going to B-17s." We never saw him again.

I remember writing my father after about twenty hours, telling him I had bailed out once, had one plane on fire, had sprung an oil leak with one, and, in another, had fuel fill the cockpit and fuselage. "Dad, this fighter pilot life is exciting and great but I don't understand how anybody gets very old doing it. It doesn't seem to be the kind of thing that one could do as a career." Little did I know that these experiences were the first of dozens of brushes with death. I managed to fly fighters twenty-eight out of my thirty years in the Air Force, and although it really did get safer the longer we flew—better navigational aids, longer runways, good approach aids in weather, and better supervision—the risk was always there.

Our group moved from Yontan to Naha in July 1947. Naha had a lot of advantages. The runway was longer and was asphalt instead of coral, living conditions were better, and there were some girls.

The initial move to Naha put me in a long Quonset hut barracks with twenty-five other people. After West Point, that was grim and my jaws tightened at the mere thought of it. Jesse Hearin, Oscar McCabe, and I decided the first day that living barracks-style with twenty-five other guys was for the birds.

We went to the northern part of Okinawa, and for a couple of bottles of whiskey we got an old abandoned Seabee hut. We put it on a flatbed and brought it back to Naha. A couple of additions later we had a neat little shack on top of the hill with a living room, three bedrooms, and a bath. We went back to the junkyards and got a record player. A P-47 drop tank on top was filled by the fire truck once a week and we had a fine gravity-feed shower. Using the junkyards again, we combined numerous Servel gas-fired refrigerators to make one that worked so we had cold sodas and ice cubes. Tapping into the main telephone lines topped it off, though every once in a while we'd get into a phone conversation with someone else and wonder who the hell it was. We got away with that for a long, long time.

The roof leaked. We replaced everything known to man on that roof, and still in a heavy rain, the water leaked to the floor below. In desperation, we tried Oscar's idea: we cut a one-foot circular hole in the floor and hinged the lid so it could be opened when it looked like rain. The idea worked perfectly. When it rained, the water fell from the roof through the hole onto the ground underneath the house and drained off. Oscar was an engineering genius.

The only drawback with our house was the presence of rats, just like in the Philippines. Every now and then you'd wake up in the middle of the night and there'd be a rat sitting on your mosquito netting a foot from your face. A good smack and the rat would go flying across the room. You could hear it hit the wall and run off into the night. Okinawa was fun.

In the fall of 1947, one of our squadrons started converting to F-80 Shooting Stars, jets! Before the whole group of pilots checked out, the question came up regarding the feasibility of getting our entire West Point bunch transitioned. Since we had all arrived at the same time and were going home in a few months. It didn't seem worth the time and effort to train pilots who would be leaving in sixty days. The group commander ended up stipulating a pilot had to have five months retainability (three more than we would have) if he was going to check out in F-80s. Three of us had to have a shot at those Lockheeds, so we extended for three months. I figured we'd dodge the old adage "If you haven't been, you can't go." Throughout my career I lived by a simple dictum—if you have a chance to check out in a new airplane, don't ever pass it up, because you never know when some guy will tell you, "I'm sorry, if you only had a little time in this airplane we'd let you fly it, but since you don't . . ."

Our CO, Colonel Boushey, gave the okay and let the three of us stay. By the time our classmates got ready to leave in January 1948, we had about twenty-five or thirty hours in the F-80. When it was time for them to get on the boat and go home, a bunch of them gave us the hee-haw, kidding us about the big party they were going to have as the ship pulled out. We may have felt a little sorry that night but the next day the Old Man called us in his office, asking if we were satisfied with our decision to stay. We all said yes, that even though our classmates were going home, we would probably do the same thing if we had to do it over again.

"You guys did pretty well in the training program. I'm going to release you. I just wanted to know who really wanted to fly jets. Pack your bags and get on the next aircraft to the States." As it turned out, a week later we were gone, arriving before our shipboard buddies. Our last laugh was really a good one.

CHAPTER 6

The Heroes

One of the biggest advantages we jet jockeys reaped from our F-80 checkout was the reassignment. All the other guys ended up going to Thunderbolts or Mustangs while the three of us got assignments to jet outfits. I was sent to the F-80–equipped 56th Fighter Group at Selfridge Field, Michigan. The outfit was full of famous aces: Dave Schilling, Gabby Gabreski, Bill Whisner, Don Adams, Bill Shomo, Frank Klibbe, Irwin Dregne, and many others. They were all heroes in WW II, but there I was, no combat experience. It made me wonder about the years I spent at West Point. Most of these guys were my age, give or take a year or two.

The flying at Selfridge was great. The F-80s were new, so everywhere we went we were the center of attention. For about ten months of the year we flew out of Selfridge; the other two months our squadron went to Oscoda Air Base in northern Michigan where we completed our annual gunnery and bombing requirements.

When we went to Oscoda, it was like a summer move. Air-ground gunnery, bombing, and air-to-air gunnery from 0600 to about 1100 when the air began to get a little choppy. By 1300 we were all at the beach. In the evening we would go to a place called Ewing's where they made the best fried chicken you ever tasted, and served all you could eat. I hope they are still in business—that place was really something.

The summer of 1948 we had a visitor come fly with us at Oscoda, Colonel Charles Lindbergh. He checked out in the F-80 and flew some gunnery missions with us. A nice guy, quiet and unassuming, he was most pleasant to be around. We were in great awe of the "Lone Eagle."

From 1939 to 1948, when I arrived at Selfridge, golf was a thing of the past. I had played a few times at the University of Denver, not at all at West Point since it conflicted with my air cadet training, and, of course, there had been no golf course on Okinawa. To enjoy golf you need a fellow nut who will go anytime, anyplace, in any weather. I found one. Captain Jim Raebel, our engineering officer, and I got to playing after work when we could. I never knew golf could be so much fun. Jim loved to bet and had an infectious laugh that could turn your arms and legs to rubber when he got going.

One evening we were playing the Selfridge nine-hole course and came to a hole that had an ammunition storage area on the right side of the fairway. I hit first and sliced my drive over the steel fence into the storage area. Amid great laughter and unwarranted promises as to how much he was going to win on the hole, Jim proceeded to put his ball into the storage area with mine.

We hit second shots, but as we approached the storage area we could see both of our balls lying out in the open between the fence and the ammo building. There were few people playing that evening, so we figured if Jim would cup his hands and give me a boost, I could get over the fence. Coming back appeared easy because of the proximity of the building to the fence. Several big red Keep Out signs notwithstanding, over the fence I went. I not only got our balls but found about thirty more. I threw the balls across the fence and scrambled back over to help divide them up.

Jim and I were sitting on the ground, selecting balls, when

Colonel Baker, the air base group commander, obviously out of breath from a long run, descended upon us. He was furious! He had seen me go over the fence, so he started in on me. After a tirade against me that seemed more like a filibuster, he suddenly became aware of James Raebel, his next-door neighbor. "And, Captain Raebel," Baker puffed out, "you are the senior officer here and it's inconceivable you would let this junior officer violate a restricted area."

With a perfectly straight face, Jim turned to me and said, "You see, you dumb son of a bitch, I told you not to go over that fence." Well, I was dumbfounded. I looked Jim in the eye with total disbelief and could see a slight trace of a smile he was holding back. I started laughing and Jim couldn't stand it any longer, either. He broke out laughing, but Colonel Baker failed to see any humor in all this. In fact, he got madder than ever, thinking we were laughing at him. It all resulted in a direct order to report to his office the next morning. It was a good thing Jim and Colonel Baker were neighbors—somehow he smoothed it over and we got off the hook.

Cross-country flights were authorized at Selfridge—you could leave Friday noon but had to be back Sunday night unless you had aircraft problems. Being single, I was gone all the time to see someone or do something. It was great. Naturally, you accomplished a lot of good navigational training, time on instruments, and bad-weather letdowns. I thanked my lucky stars many times for the experience I gained banging around the good old U.S.A. in that F-80.

Many of those weekends I went to Long Beach, California, to see Dotty, the gal I met on Okinawa. She and I gradually became more serious about each other as the summer sped by, and before long we were talking about getting married. She had planned to take a tour in Alaska, working for the Civil Service, but I was able to change her mind and we were married in Belmont Shores, California, on 18 September 1948. After our honeymoon, we got a modest set of Air Force quarters at

Selfridge and began to live what we certainly thought at the time was the good life. My first son, Kent Corbin Blesse, was born 28 January 1950.

Other than routine flying, the next year or so had only a few memorable events. In the summer of 1949, Colonel Dave Schilling led sixteen of us to Germany on an exercise called Fox Able Two. It was a great trip—Newfoundland, Iceland, Greenland, Scotland, and Germany. I tried to make the 56th Group gunnery team in early 1950 but was dropped on the last cut before the meet. I was crushed, but it was good experience. The 56th Group began converting to F-86s that spring and I became involved in ferrying them from California to Michigan for several months. Then, suddenly, the Korean War burst upon the scene, 25 June 1950.

At that time I had about 1,200 hours in the F-80, 120 in the F-86, 700 in the P-47, and a few more in the P-40 and P-51, so I was better prepared for combat than most of the lads who went off to World War II. During my five years in fighters so far, I found I could gain an advantage in a dogfight but never could win in the debriefing room. When you got back it didn't matter how bad your opponent was or what he did; if he had flown combat in the war, it was always a shrug of the shoulders and a casual remark like "Well, that's okay, but we just don't do it that way in combat." That was the ultimate statement I couldn't argue with. There was nothing I could say, and I wasn't going to teach him anything, because he wasn't going to listen. I made up my mind, one way or another I was going to get over there and get some combat experience, then I could look a guy in the eye and say, "Well, we just don't do it that way in combat."

In early July 1950, a requirement for a Mustang (now redesignated F-51) pilot came through the 56th Group. No one in that F-86 outfit wanted any part of it. I had a little '51 time from Hunter Field and we had a Mustang at Selfridge we used to chase parts, so I got a little more time in that one. I had never done anything but just fly around, but that seven or eight hours in the F-51 looked good in my logbook. When the requirement came down I decided this was the thing for me. I went over to Personnel and was told I'd have to have the group commander's permission, so I set off to buttonhole Colonel Gabreski. I found him the next morning and intercepted him jogging in the parking lot. I introduced myself and explained what I wanted to do. "You're making a big mistake, Blesse. If the war expands, the big show is going to be in Europe again and you don't want to get yourself stuck over in the Pacific."

Though I was young, I followed my instincts, just as I had when checking out in the F-80 and spoke up: "Sir, if I had your combat time and had shot down as many airplanes, I could afford to wait, but I can't afford to be wrong on this one. I'm a paperhanger who has never hung any paper. I'm a career officer and I really need some combat time."

Gabby, as I got to know him in later years, was always one who liked to see aggressiveness in a person. "If you feel that strongly about it, I'll give you my permission." I hotfooted it back to Personnel, got the F-51 slot, and was reassigned almost immediately to Nellis AFB, Nevada, for Mustang training. After thirty days' leave, I reported for duty, along with three other guys from tactical units, to find out Nellis had given away all F-51s. The course was conducted using the F-80.

The other three were Fred Hudson, a '49 West Point graduate; Fred Webster, a World War II fighter pilot; and Ben Sanford, a hell of a good guy who became a close friend. Ben was married to a lovely gal named Christina. During our time at Nellis I never made a pass at her, but she was extremely attractive and I always felt uncomfortable or ungainly in her presence . . . something about her just unnerved me.

With 1,200 hours in the Shooting Star, I didn't need the refresher, and neither did the other three. The Nellis instructors flew with each of us, and when they saw we could fly formation, aerobatics, qualify on the gunnery range, and do a number of other things inexperienced pilots wouldn't have been able to do, they decided to graduate us early. Most of the others at Nellis were what we called Blue Flamers, coming from desk or staff jobs without flying consistently for a year or two, so they really needed four months.

The grim reality of war was here. At last, I was on my way to my first combat tour. It would have been nice to know if I was going to fly F-80s or F-51s, but, frankly, it didn't matter to me as long as I got into combat.

CHAPTER 7

Korea

Leaving for Korea in October 1950, I couldn't help feeling anxious about things. The war was going all our way by that time and MacArthur was talking about having everyone back home by Christmas. I was all for that as long as I got into it before it was over.

The Korean War was two wars fought in several different phases. From 25 June to 25 November 1950 was one distinct phase. From the latter part of June through most of August, the UN forces were backed all the way down to the end of the peninsula by the North Koreans. The South Korean Army had collapsed and it looked as if we would lose everything. President Truman decided we were not going to abandon Korea; more American troops were committed, and after some tough times, things stabilized around the Pusan perimeter. It stayed like that until mid-September when MacArthur landed at Inchon. He directed a breakout the next day and began an operation that cut off the major portion of the North Korean Army. Tens of thousands of prisoners were taken, and in about ten days the war started to disintegrate.

On 29 September, MacArthur and Republic of Korea (ROK) President Syngman Rhee held a victory parade in Seoul, which had been recaptured, an event hailed as the end of the war. The allied command changed the rules at that point. Instead of simply getting our territory back, the UN seized the opportunity to unify all of Korea.

Communist China had warned us through our envoy in Switzerland and through other channels that if we crossed the 38th parallel, she would fight. MacArthur ignored the rhetoric and decided to press for the Yalu River. On 25 November, just about the time his forces got there, China entered the war.

In the last part of October, the four of us found ourselves at Johnson AFB, Japan. The USAF personnel replacement center told us it would be a two- or three-month wait; seems all the people ahead were F-80–trained as well! "Most of them are younger than you guys and haven't flown anything but F-80s, so they aren't qualified to go to the F-51 units."

We thought about that for a while, talking it over in the club. Out of the bunch only Ben Sanford and Fred Webster had seen combat, a tour in Europe during World War II flying the Mustang, which Ben called the Spam Can. Ben was adamant—he was not going back to war in the Spam Can no matter what. As the evening wore on, several drinks later, we had Ben on top of the moon telling war stories. We wanted to stick together, so by 2300 we got him to agree that maybe going back to war in a P-51 wasn't all that bad.

The next day we went over and signed up. Twenty-four hours later we found ourselves in the back of a C-119, on the way to Pusan, South Korea, the main base of the 18th Fighter-Bomber Group. The group had two squadrons of Mustangs. There were no other passengers, but there was quite a load of cargo which apparently had not been loaded too carefully. When we landed at Pusan, the pilot dropped the big bird in from about ten feet—it was like jumping out of a two-story building. The booms on the fuselage bent and dropped all the way down to the runway! When I rotated home after my first tour, I departed from Pusan and that C-119 was still sitting on the side of the field.

I didn't feel any better coming into the combat theater that way, but I forgot about it with the warm welcome from the squadron. One of the guys, Captain Joe Lane, who turned out to be my flight leader, came down to meet us and said, "Are we glad to see you! We only have seven pilots. We need you on tomorrow morning's mission, but before you fly you have to have a regular theater combat checkout. That requires three hours' flying in the P-51 and ten landings." It was 1100, and without missing a beat he went on. "You're scheduled for 1300, so let the sergeant take your bags and he'll get them down to your tent. Let's get to the mess hall for some chow and I'll give you a briefing while we're down there."

By one o'clock I found myself in a little ole '51 flying around Pusan Air Base having a good time, getting used to the airplane again. It was "clean," no drop tanks or ordnance, so it was just like I remembered. I had yet to fly one that even had external fuel tanks on it. After an hour, Joe Lane joined up and had me fly formation, making sure I wouldn't be a hazard to him in the combat zone. Convinced I could handle that, he turned me loose. "Go back to the traffic pattern and shoot your ten landings," he said. I did that in reasonable fashion, then made my way to the mess hall for chow. Joe was there and he began filling me in on what to expect the next day.

"Tomorrow morning—now don't worry about this—they'll come around about 0300 and wake you up. I've been here a long time and have never flown at night—the instruments are not suitable. If you get caught in the weather, all you've got is an attitude gyro, which tumbles at sixty degrees. If you hit any rough air, you're really in some deep, serious trouble. We try to avoid weather flying also because, in addition to a limited-capability attitude indicator, you don't have very good navigational equipment. We have to be able to know where we're going at all times and that means seeing the ground. The only navigational instrument we have is a Detrola ADF which gets pretty confusing since the needle points the same way traveling toward the station as it does going away from it. It really only tells you if the station is left or right. When the war started, some night missions were flown, but several losses to darkness and weather made even the most aggressive commanders write it off as a bad idea.

"Anyway, when they wake you up, it'll be a good chance to go down to the briefing room, talk to the escape-and-evasion people, get basic procedures down, and get the call signs for the day. About that time Joint Operations Center (JOC) will cancel our mission and you can go back to bed."

Precisely at the stroke of three, 11 November 1950, I was shaken awake. "Come on, Captain, it's time to go to the briefing." We trudged down the path, went through the briefing to hit targets north of Pyongyang, heard the escape/evasion bit, then waited for the JOC to call and cancel the mission. For some reason that morning, JOC didn't cancel it right away. Joe Lane shrugged his shoulders. "It's raining out there, ceiling about 400 feet, so it won't hurt anything to go out and preflight the airplanes. That'll be good for you, because you won't get a chance to preflight in the dark too often. Take your flashlight, do this thing right, and you'll be all set later in the day when the weather improves."

Pyongyang was the capitol of North Korea. MacArthur's 8th and 10th Armies had already driven north, racing to the Yalu River, and it looked as if everything was going great for the United Nations cause. We were supposed to hit our targets, then land at Pyongyang East, a 3,900-foot cornfield with no facilities—just some people to load rockets, napalm, ammo, and fuel. The idea was to refuel and rearm, take off immediately, contact another controller, and hit the next enemy position. The 18th Group was supposed to have the nice 6,000-foot concrete runway about ten miles west, but the Eighth Group somehow got there first and we ended up with the cornfield. We went out, preflighted, and still had no call from JOC. Into the aircraft, roll the canopy shut to ward off the misty rain, get all squared away with parachute and harness sitting in a cold, soaked flight suit . . . no call. We started up, checked in on the radio, and still there was no call. Joe's voice was an octave higher—we were going to taxi to the end of the runway in the dark, then he'd call JOC and let them know we weren't supposed to be doing this.

The bumpy pierced-steel planking (PSP) taxiway and runway had thousands of circular holes that allowed mud to ooze through, which slimed the steel that bore the weight of the aircraft. This was totally new to me. The long nose and low tailwheel of the P-51 robs the pilot of all forward view until the tail comes up on takeoff. You can't taxi straight ahead or you'll run over somebody, or something, so you S-turn left and right, to look out each side. Even trying to S-turn, we were sliding on the PSP—it really didn't look like this thing was going to be habit-forming.

Holding short of the active runway, fearless leader couldn't raise JOC, so he called our command post and had them check. The return message was a jolt. "They need you. There's a forward air controller just north of Pyongyang—plenty of trouble up there this morning—and they need you at first light. *Go!*"

At that last word, my heart went right up underneath my tongue, thoughts bouncing all over the inside of my head. I didn't want my first loaded takeoff in a P-51 to be at night in the rain. I had never flown a propeller-driven fighter at night and this didn't seem to be the way to start. I pushed up my resolve and thought something silly like, I guess this is why I get flying pay.

The first mistake I made (after waking up at 0300) was lining up on my leader's wing for a formation takeoff. Since the guys hadn't been flying at night, they didn't know enough to tell me that this was a bad deal. As soon as Joe started to push the throttle forward, I knew I had made one of the most serious errors of my life.

The P-51 had a 12-cylinder, 1,695-HP Merlin engine with exhaust pipes that shot hot fire all the way down the side of the nose in the form of a big, bright light. Bright lights destroy night vision, and mine was gone. I sat there flying on that piece of flame without seeing an airplane or knowing whether I was going up or down or where his wings were. I mean I could see nothing. When the ball of fire started moving up, I moved up; when it moved down, I moved down. About forty-five minutes into the mission, it began to get lighter, the clouds thinned, and we broke out of the overcast. I started to feel a lot better. In fact, the thought struck me I might live through this yet.

As we flew through North Korea, Joe checked in with "Boxcar," our forward air controller (FAC). Boxcar came back quickly: "I've got some good targets for you this morning. Watch where I put this rocket." I saw the rocket impact but he radioed, "It didn't hit exactly where I wanted it. Target is about fifty meters to the right." We made a pass, dropped our napalm, and blew up some things—it looked great. The FAC gave us another target, which we strafed, but before we had finished our runs, we got a call relayed through some other aircraft. "The command post says for you guys to go back to Pyongyang East—it's getting hazy as hell." My first combat mission was turning out to be a real corker . . . but it wasn't over yet.

Joe made one circle to get us together and off we went for Pyongyang East, about ten minutes away. There were no clouds, it was just a thick layer of haze. Visibility was terrible, officially listed as a tenth of a mile, which means you could see about five hundred feet on a slant. We peeled off over the field in the proper order to land. I was flying number two, where the weakest guy is placed, since this was my first mission. Joe made a circle of the field. I followed with good spacing and things looked fine. The problem was, we couldn't find the end of the cornfield, and by the time we saw it, we were too far down to land. We repeated this fiasco about three or four times.

There was a pilot sitting in a Mustang on the ground acting as a tower. He could see what was happening and we told him the visibility was too poor to get things sorted out. He had some people put about twenty gallons of oil in two fifty-five-gallon drums and had them placed on the end of the field. They ignited the oil and two columns of black smoke came up from the end of the runway. After one more practice pass, the leader said we could land on the next go-around. He peeled off and turned on downwind; spacing was good and we continued on final approach.

As I came in on short final, I watched Joe touch down and begin his landing roll. Just as his tail was about to settle, I touched down and I could still see him clearly. Suddenly, out of the corner of my eye, I saw a 6x6 truck. This 3,900-foot runway was short, with terrible weather all around, so the three people in the truck were absolutely sure no one in his right mind would ever try to land there. They were merrily crossing the runway to do something important like get to the other side.

My first thought was, Joe is going to hit that truck! Then he went out of sight. The 6x6 was still in plain view . . . it then became crystal clear to me who the hell was going to hit that truck. With so little time to do what I needed to do, maybe a second and a half, I hit full right rudder and right brake. I was at that very awkward speed where the '51 was too slow to go around and too fast to ground-loop. Almost unconsciously my hand darted out, turning the battery and mag switch off. My left wing hit the cab of the truck, swinging me around, accelerating the right wing and causing the aircraft to try to fly again. The next thing I knew, I was looking straight down at the corn patch at what seemed like 90°.

My stricken bird came down and started to cartwheel—nose first, then wingtip, then tail, about three times. I could see rockets being lobbed off in all directions—we'd never had a chance to use them. With a great thumping crunch, the '51 came to rest upside down, trapping me underneath. I gingerly checked out my fingers and toes, felt around, found no blood. Hell, I wasn't even hurt!

My next thought was getting out since gas started dripping

on me from the fuselage tank—it was hitting me in the back, rolling down and collecting in my P-1 helmet. This was a football-type flying helmet, not the soft cloth variety most pilots wore. Two guys came running over and began digging a hole under the canopy. I released my harness and fell into the hole, almost breaking my neck. I never even felt it. I came out of there like a scared rabbit and ran about a hundred yards before stopping to look back. A mist was coming up from the airplane, gas fumes which did not stop for two and a half hours, but that aircraft never burned.

I strolled over to a nearby tent marked Operations. A major sat at a table reading something or other and without looking up he said, "Have a little trouble out there?"

"Yeah, it didn't go too good."

"Did you get hurt?"

"No, don't believe so."

"Do you want to fly anymore?"

"Sure, that's what I came for," I replied.

"Fine. In the next tent there are three pilots briefing to fly. They need a fourth. Go join 'em. The haze is burning off now, so you should be able to get off in twenty or thirty minutes."

Within twenty minutes I was in another F-51 on my second combat mission. Looking back, I was glad it happened that way. An accident in peacetime generally results in grounding the pilot until the accident board meets. It can be a month or more. By that time the pilot has had a chance to think it over, relive it time and again in his mind, and maybe get to the point where he doesn't want to continue flying. I had no time to think. That first day was rugged flying out of Pyongyang East— seven major accidents on the field in thirty-five minutes. We just kept on flying, and things smoothed out as the weather improved somewhat and we got a little more experience.

One of the maddening aspects of flying out of Pyongyang was "Bedcheck Charlie," a Russian-designed Po-2 biplane which came over in the middle of the night to keep us awake. For all I know he had someone in the backseat who tossed little bombs over the side. That thing would fly over in the dark at about 70 knots, hitting airplanes, tents, and whatever else was in the open with his small bombs. It was a long time before anyone got that guy. We heard an F-94 did the job but it was a midair collision. The controllers tracked him on radar and saw the interceptor accidentally fly into him. That was the end of Bedcheck Charlie but at the high price of two damned good fighter pilots and an expensive aircraft.

Before long, I had ten missions, then fifteen, and finally twenty. About every twenty missions, a pilot's flying was evaluated—what had been accomplished, his reaction to combat, and whether or not an Air Medal was in order. It seems living through a crash met the criteria, so I got my first decoration. Eventually I received twenty other Air Medals, many of which didn't come that easy.

I thought things were going well. Then I heard about the "black hat." Each squadron was required to supply a pilot to the ground forces as a FAC. He would sit on the ground with a radio during a firefight and direct the fighters where they were needed. A normal tour was thirty days, so when a new FAC was needed, a meeting was held and the "black hat" was dragged out. Everyone with twenty to ninety missions put his name in the hat, and at the stroke of midnight, the squadron commander would draw a name. It's not hard to guess whose name came out. I was very distressed, to put it mildly, especially after I learned that the previous FAC was wounded when the Chinese attacked his position one night.

I was given five men and three vehicles, including an M39 armored personnel carrier without a top but with excellent ability to stop bullets as long as one didn't hang over the side. The other two vehicles were jeeps stuffed with radio equipment, maintained by the radio operator.

On the way to the front we went through Kimpo Air Base in Seoul, where some friends of mine from Selfridge, including a squadron commander, were flying F-80s. I asked him if I could go on a mission with them. "Sure, come on," he said. So I sent the guys to the NCO club and went to the briefing. It was near the end of November just after the Chinese entered the war. The 8th Army, cut off by the Chinese while trying to reach the Yalu River, was trying to retreat. The 2d Division was positioned along a railroad and a main highway, holding the enemy back so the rest of the American units could retreat gracefully. It took too long for some to get around. When the 2d Division tried to withdraw, the hills along both sides of the road were full of Chinese gun positions.

When our flight of F-80s got up there, the Mosquito AT-6 FAC had been shot down, which left no one to direct the strike. We started down the road looking for any sign of life but didn't see anything. Suddenly we came upon a long line of vehicles heading south twenty-five to fifty yards apart, filled with GIs, arms and legs dangling over the sides. They had obviously been caught in an ambush. When the first few vehicles were shot up, it stopped movement and a slaughter took place on the five-mile-long stretch. I have never seen anything that left me with such a desolate feeling. I was glad when the mission was over—now it was time to go to work as a forward air controller for the Army.

Certainly, my time with the Army was interesting, but I was jumpy all the time. I had been trained to fight in the air, but being on the ground, not knowing exactly where you were all the time, constantly on the move, left me with an uneasy feeling. It was the same for the Army people when they were in our world. We took several of them on some relatively safe missions, and afterward in the briefing room, they could hardly get a cup of coffee to their lips without spilling it. It's just a matter of what you are trained to do. When the unknown sneaks in, it brings uncertainty, doubt, and a mild form of fear with it. Mild, you know, like "Let's get the hell out of here."

The regimental commander didn't exactly fill me with confidence . . . "Listen, Captain, there's only one thing I want to tell you. Keep those goddamn vehicles pointed south and warm them up every two hours during the night.'' That's all he had to say. Those engines were never cold. I think I used more fuel as a forward air controller keeping those engines warm than I did later on as a fighter pilot. Unlike my predecessor, the time with the Army was relatively inactive and uneventful, but I didn't know it was going to be that way until it was over.

When I got back to the 67th Squadron, I took my first shower in thirty days. God, it was great! With the Army, I had a nice little helmet in which I heated water on a potbellied stove; when it got hot enough, that was my bath. I couldn't get in, but it got me wet.

The squadron was flying out of Suwon, just south of Seoul. As I returned in the first week of January 1951, a much wiser victim of the ''black hat,'' the lines were crumbling with all units falling back. The whole fighter group would have to move to Chinhae on the south tip of Korea. The next afternoon I got in an F-51 and went south with everyone else as the base was being evacuated. Kimpo, just north of Suwon, was getting the same treatment. We were going to lose it again.

Arrival at Chinhae was depressing. The base was anything but plush; everyone was in tents. It was bitterly cold, which gave us a whole new problem in the event we were shot down. Flying clothes were heavy and bulky, and anything substantial enough to keep you warm was too heavy to move in on the ground. It was one of those times, and there were lots of them, when we just shrugged and said that's what we get flying pay for.

The South Africans had a squadron of F-51s on the base. They were damn good pilots, well respected by all the other combat units. They were a fun-loving lot, constantly holding wild parties in their officers' club. The morning after would always find those not flying repairing the club, the furniture, and everything else broken the night before.

The airfield at Chinhae had been destroyed earlier in the war, before we got there. A huge hangar at the end of the runway had been reduced to assorted twisted I-beams, and the water at the end of the relatively short runway invited you back to Japan, where the runways were long, nobody shot at you, the sheets were clean, and the O club was in full swing every night.

I flew another forty missions or so out of Chinhae before I got shot up pretty bad. A FAC put us on what he called a "lucrative target." The North Koreans must have thought so, too, because it was quite well defended. Four of us were working over the target, coordinating our individual passes to provide cover for the aircraft making the attack. While protecting another Mustang, I got caught in a crossfire of quad .50 caliber guns. Suddenly I was leaking gas, oil, hydraulic fluid, and just about everything. My first thought was the coolant tank: If it has been hit, I'll be down in a couple of minutes. No coolant, no engine, simple as that. A hundred thoughts tried to burst their way out of my head. If I go down, where's the best terrain to try to put the aircraft down? Where are other enemy troops? Are there places for me to hide? Can I move on the ground? What's my best escape route? The engine seems to be running okay. By then I was fifteen miles east and with each smooth revolution of that engine, my composure was improving. Finally, twenty minutes later, I popped up over the last hill and saw the airfield at Taegu. It wasn't much, but it sure looked good to me.

I had to remain at Taegu for three or four days while they repaired forty-two holes in my airplane, plus some assorted damage to the hydraulic and fuel systems. During that time I met Colonel Murphy, CO of the F-80 group operating out of Taegu. He was to change the direction of my first combat tour in Korea.

Colonel Murphy knew me from Selfridge. One evening at the club he asked if I'd like to come to Taegu and fly jets again.

"Yes sir, I'd like that. I've got close to seventy missions now and feel like I've caught up for not making World War II. I'd like to see what the jet war is like."

That's all he needed: "Okay, I'm always getting P-51 pilots that I have to transition and train, getting little use of them for six weeks. When I get the next one, I'll make arrangements with your group commander to make a swap."

A couple of weeks later, the CO of the 18th Fighter Group called me in. If I could find a way up to Taegu, my transfer was all set. I hitched a ride on a cargo bird and the next day was in Taegu for indoctrination in flying F-80s with the 49th Fighter-Bomber Group. I joined the 7th Squadron for a quick transition, then was scheduled to take over a flight.

With 1,200 hours in the airplane, I was spared some details. I was told to get in, shoot a couple of landings, and then I'd be ready for combat. Sounded good to me, though I hated having to fly off that damned pierced-steel planking. The Air Force must have covered Korea from one end to the other with the stuff. After a few missions, newly laid PSP would sink down in waves or humps, and a hump at the wrong time tended to throw the airplane into the air a little early. Suck back on the stick at the wrong time and you could kill a hell of a lot of precious airspeed. You just had to let it go like a truck on a very rough road until you felt you had enough airspeed to fly.

Taegu's runway amounted to about 6,000 feet of PSP—just barely enough to get a combat-loaded F-80 airborne with precious little to spare, provided the temperatures weren't too high.

On my first flight out of Taegu, I nearly busted my ass. I went across the PSP in that F-80, hippity-hippity-hop, banging up and down. Almost halfway down the runway I noticed the throttle had vibrated back slightly and that I didn't have full power. In an '80, which took forever to accelerate at one hundred percent power, each percent of full power lost made a drastic difference in your ability to make a safe takeoff.

I shoved the throttle back to one hundred percent. I was too far down the runway to try to stop. I let that thing run all the

way until it looked like I didn't have more than a hundred feet
to spare. This was going to be a dust-sniffer test for sure. (We
used to joke about the F-80's lack of power. We all claimed
Lockheed had put a dust sniffer in the nosewheel well so the
bird wouldn't fly till it sniffed the dirt at the far end of the
runway.) Barely cracking the nosewheel off, I eased back on
the stick, pulled up the landing gear, and prayed it would fly.
I couldn't tell if it was going to settle back in or not—it just
stayed there without climbing. Disaster was so close I could
feel it rise in my throat. I felt like my ass was dragging in the
Korean dirt. "Come on, baby, don't settle back in now.
There's no runway under you!"

Just as it began to seem I was going to make it, the
thought hit me. The wires! Christ, the wires! About three
quarters of a mile off the end of the runway was a power line
with wires about seventy-five feet off the ground. Hanging
there, a gnat's ass above stalling, I didn't have enough power
to climb over the lines. I couldn't do anything—one abrupt
move on the stick and the jet would have stalled, slamming
me back into the ground. It wasn't as though I had a choice.
I stayed on the deck and flew underneath those damn power
lines. A few thousand feet later, I had picked up enough airspeed to begin climbing and the world looked a lot brighter.
Thank you, Lady Luck!

The rest of the flight was routine. Transition goals were met,
and in one flight, I was combat-ready in the F-80. Later, when
I mentioned the power loss to another pilot, he said, "Didn't
you know that aircraft has a bad throttle friction knob?" This
tiny circular hand nut on the throttle quadrant keeps the throttle
from drifting back when you remove your hand. Seems several
aircraft in the squadron had knobs that didn't work too well.
Nobody had thought to tell me about it, and though it seems
like a small item, if there had been a full load of bombs and
ammunition on the aircraft, I would have undoubtedly bought
the ranch right there. I should have checked. Relying on other
people in this business can kill you.

I got in thirty-five relatively uneventful F-80 missions, which put me over the hundred mark, and my tour was suddenly over. I was kind of excited about going back to the States a combat veteran. I had plenty of time to think about it. They sent me home by boat, which went over like a sewer cover with me.

CHAPTER 8

Between Tours

After finally making it Stateside, I was assigned to a fighter group at Moses Lake, Washington, but that group was going to England, and since I was a recent combat returnee, I couldn't go. They gave me a choice—Albuquerque, New Mexico, or George AFB, California. A phone call told me my date of rank would make me a flight commander at George so I chose that. Besides, I would go to the 94th Squadron—Rickenbacker's old "Hat in the Ring" outfit dating from 1918. That had to be pretty good.

George was a good base about a hundred miles from Los Angeles, and the desert weather always provided clear skies and forty-mile visibility. They were flying F-86s, which I thought was great. I had flown Sabres at Selfridge a few years before and was glad to be back flying the best that the USAF had to offer.

As I settled in at George, who should show up but Ben Sanford, assigned to the 94th from his combat tour in F-51s. Though Ben had been hurt when he bellied a Mustang into a rice paddy, he was back on flying status and we quickly filled in all the blank spaces since I left the 67th at Chinhae. Of course, there was Christine, Ben's wife, more beautiful even than I remembered her. Typical of any Air Force base, there were plenty of social events where we kept running into each other. After a while, I had a hunch she felt about me the same way I did about her, but at that time we never said anything about it. From our first meeting in September 1950, we began a seventeen-year relationship that stretched halfway around the world and was finally left smoldering in a sea of indecision. She was one of the finest ladies I ever met.

In July 1951 the 94th was full of characters: Lou Green, a super guy with worlds of operational experience who would get two MiGs in Korea; Les Arasmith, smart and capable with the best sense of humor I've ever seen; Ben Sanford, very capable operationally and dubbed the "River Boat Gambler" because of his willingness to wager; Joe McConnell, my assistant flight commander, who later became the top jet ace in Korea; Ralph Parr, who was destined to become a double jet ace after an air-ground tour in F-80s; Houston Tuel, outstanding fighter pilot and instructor and who but for the toss of the dice would certainly have been one of the leading MiG killers. He got three as it was. The squadron was packed with good people.

The facilities were good for a fighter squadron—good hangars and operations building with ample space for off-duty activity. Colonel Walker Mahurin remembered some things about our squadron besides flying:

"They had a Ping-Pong table set up in the pilot's ready room, which was a lean-to off the side of a big hangar at George, so there was an almost constant Ping-Pong game in progress. Boots seemed to be one of the better players (if not the best). The pilots often played for small bets, and another flight leader named Ben Sanford seemed to challenge Boots more than anyone else. Ben always lost. It finally got to the point where Ben owed Boots around $7,500. I was in the ready room when Ben offered to bet Boots double or nothing. Boots won. Ben then offered to bet his car against the debt. Boots won. Ben then slammed his car keys on the table and offered to bet Boots his (Ben's) wife against the debt. Boots won. The last I saw of both of them, Boots drove past Ben who was walking down the street and yelled out that he was on his way to Ben's house to collect the bet. Of course it was all in fun, but Ben didn't take it lightly."

The flying at George was great. An F-51 wing was there, so gradually we learned what to do and not to do when fighting a propeller-driven fighter. That came in handy later on. Most of our flying was intercepts, which served as great training for what was to come later for me. Even before I left Korea the first time, I asked about transferring to a combat F-86 wing. I was told it was impossible and that I had to go back to the States and get in the Western Air Defense Command, then volunteer to come back. It so happened George AFB fit into that category perfectly, and hardly a day went by that I didn't think about returning to Korea. But I forgot about everything for a while in the summer of 1951.

The National Air Races were being held, and General Electric was sponsoring a race from Chicago to Detroit. It was decided the race would be flown by F-86s, and two USAF outfits were chosen to supply pilots, aircraft, and ground crews. The 94th Squadron somehow became one of the two units and, since all the pilots wanted a chance to participate, we drew straws to determine who would go. Captain Earl Richmond and I ended up being the lucky winners to represent the 94th and immediately began planning for the race that we hoped would make us a winner.

Each of us was assigned our own F-86 and crew chief. We reported to Chicago a week early to shine them up, make our flight plans, and decide how we were going to run the race. The course was only about 280 miles long. That was close enough to almost make it on the deck without external fuel tanks, but not quite. Two other pilots from other squadrons were in the race as well. Captain Pappy Liles was one of them, and we were to do a lot of flying together in the next five or six years.

We all had Sabres, so we knew it was going to be close. The central decision revolved around flying slower with drop tanks, skipping a climb to altitude and going all out on the deck, or climbing to around 12,000 feet without tanks, then letting down when close to the finish.

During that week, we all made the flight several times, using different techniques. One of the four pilots was going on the deck with tanks. The other three of us elected to leave the tanks off, go to 10 or 15,000 feet, stay at a hundred percent power with a little better fuel consumption, and then drop down. I tried it several times, first going to 15,000 feet, which left me with quite a bit of fuel. The next time I dropped it to 12 and still had too much fuel. After trying at 9,000 feet, I finally had it pegged around 8,500. That left me thirty gallons of fuel to land—one try.

Our instructions on finishing were to hit the boundary of the airfield, make a 90° left turn, and cross the finish line, which was actually parallel to our line of flight. We contested that but they couldn't change it. At least, that's the last word two of us got. The other two guys got a call midway between Chicago and Detroit to skip that procedure and just come straight across the field, never mind the 90° turn. We didn't hear it because we had our radios tuned to a different channel.

At best, there wasn't ten seconds between all these race flight profiles. As fate would have it, I was leading about eight or ten plane lengths ahead of number two with the other pair directly behind him. The drop-tank Sabre was last, one of the lucky ones to receive the change in plans. We were all down to about 1,000 feet and screaming in with no more than 200 yards between me and number four. At that speed (I was clocked at 687 mph), we were only split seconds apart as we approached the field boundary. Two of us started the left turn, as originally planned, while the other two went straight for the new finish line. Why there wasn't a massive four-way collision I'll never know, but somehow we missed each other; like the Thunderbirds, but unplanned.

There was a heated discussion afterward about who actually won the race. Earl Richmond said he was the winner, and he certainly had a point since he was the first to cross the revised finish line (he was the third to cross the field boundary). They finally awarded the thing to me because I crossed the field boundary first and would have been the first to cross either finish line. Anyway, I got a real nice watch, inscribed on the back *Capt. F. C. Blesse, National Air Races 1951, 687.142 mph.*

Shortly after our return from the Air Races, we got a new group commander, Walker "Bud" Mahurin. He was about my age, but he was busy shooting down aircraft while I was still at West Point. Bud didn't look old enough to be a colonel, but behind that young face was a man blessed with superb hand-to-eye coordination and an aggressive nature that made him one of the leading aces of the European theater. He ran up a string of twenty victories, and his aggressive, likable personableness made him a role model for young aspiring fighter pilots.

As fate would have it, Bud was assigned to our squadron for checkout in the F-86, and then to my flight where I personally conducted his training. That association with him on a personal basis was among the best things that ever happened to me. It had a profound influence on my career, not to mention a friendship it started between us, initially based on mutual respect, that has continued to grow as the years roll by. At the time of Bud's checkout I had at least two hundred hours in the F-86, so the very unorthodox training that followed left me with an appreciation for his leadership and flying ability that said, "Anytime, anyplace, you lead, I'll follow."

Needless to say, Colonel Mahurin wasn't quite as impressed as I was, and commented concerning his arrival:

"I first met Boots when he was assigned as a flight commander in the 94th Fighter-Interceptor Squadron at George

AFB. At the time, I was brand-new commander of the 1st Fighter-Interceptor Group then under Air Defense Command. The 94th Squadron had F-86As.

"Most of the pilots in the squadron had returned from the Korean War as had Boots, Les Arasmith, and a number of others. Boots had been flying F-51s in Korea, so the F-86 was a real hot dog of the period. I had been stationed in the Pentagon before being transferred to George AFB, so I had very little jet time in anything, let alone the F-86. At the time the squadron was standing alert with two aircraft on five minutes, and two on backup, and we were running intercepts on anything that penetrated the ADIZ (Air Defense Identification Zone) in our area. We also were doing aerial and ground gunnery and all the other things a squadron does to fill in the squares.

"When I met Boots, I was impressed with the fact that he looked very young. I didn't have an opportunity to look over his records and wasn't aware that he had graduated from the Academy. All I knew was that he led a flight and was a very keen competitor in almost anything. That included dogfighting in the F-86."

The Boy Colonel was eager to start flying and I got on with it as quickly as possible. The regulations for checkout were laid out in our wing directives, and the first two missions were conducted in strict compliance. During the second debriefing, the colonel asked when we were going to start flying the aircraft. I told him we had to follow the directives and that the kind of flying he was referring to came many hours down the road—"unless, of course, the colonel wished a transition program designed strictly for him." The colonel wished.

Missions three through ten were like no other in any checkout program I've ever heard of. I started gingerly, not knowing how much recent flying Colonel Mahurin had been doing. We flew some formation and it was obvious he needed very little practice, so I had him drop into what we called trail formation. That was me leading and his aircraft about fifty feet behind me. The object in this drill was to do turns, dives, and rolls slow and easy in such a manner that he could stay with me. It resembled the work you see the aerobatic teams do. When a pilot mastered that, and it took a few flights, we moved him back into extended tail, where the objective was exactly the opposite. Here he was about five hundred feet back and you increased the severity of each maneuver until he could no longer stay with you. Usually, a dozen missions or so were required before any reasonable semblance of proficiency began to appear.

Not so with the Boy Colonel. We flew trail for five or ten minutes. I watched in my mirror for any slowness to react, but all I saw was an aircraft whose nose appeared to be stuffed up my tail pipe. This was mission three, and already we were past mission eight in the wing directives.

I thought a flight indoctrination to extended trail would, if nothing else, make the colonel feel we were beginning to "fly the aircraft." I gave him a few 2-G turns, light pullups, wingovers, then some easy rolls, watching him in the mirror to see where he started to have trouble. But there was no trouble. I tightened up the turns a bit—3 Gs, then 3 ½ Gs, glanced in the mirror, put my hand on the mirror to see if someone had put an F-86 decal on it—he was solid as a rock. I had taken people fifteen missions and been unable to get them as far as he had gone in twenty minutes. Another step—4 Gs, slow turn reversals, faster turn reversal, quick turn reversals. Finally, I swung him slightly to the outside and quickly reversed into him so our canopies were closer to each other than any other part of the aircraft. Bud quickly countered that, throwing me on the defensive again. "Christ, this guy's not human!" A series of turns, reversals, counter reversals followed with no one achieving any kind of firing position until we descended canopy to canopy through 10,000 feet. I called it off, motioned him into formation, and we flew home.

On the way back I thought, You dumb bastard, maneuvering like that with a guy on his third ride in the airplane and the new group commander, too. He's going to chew your ass three ways from Sunday when he gets in the briefing room. We parked side by side on the ramp, and before his engine had wound down, the colonel had his helmet off and was coming down the ladder on a bee line for my aircraft. He got about twenty feet from me, burst into a big grin, and said, "Jesus Christ, Boots, now we're really getting something done!" We recounted the flight, all rank forgotten for the moment, like a couple of new lieutenants savoring every maneuver and counter maneuver. I thought about it again driving home—three missions! Christ, what is tomorrow going to be like!

Tomorrow and tomorrow and tomorrow—they were all alike. Fight, fight, fight. Bud needed no training. He needed only a bare minimum of hours in the F-86 to transfer what he already knew from the many hours of combat flying he got while I was sitting on my ass at West Point. And so the program went—no one winning, no one losing, always fighting, both of us scaring ourselves occasionally trying to get some small advantage from something untried till that moment. The results were always the same: canopy to canopy, each trying to slow just a little without stalling, trying in vain to get behind the other. Combat flying was never as challenging. The decision in combat, except on one or two occasions, was always reached long before you arrived at the canopy to canopy phase. It was the best air-to-air combat flying I ever had, and Bud still delights in reminding me he only had a few hours against the several hundred I had. He thinks it would be easy now. Maybe he's right—but I doubt it. He recalls our missions with the same enthusiasm:

"As a newcomer to jet aviation, I tried to jump on the other pilots in the squadron every time I found them in the air. I not only learned more about the F-86, but I also learned more about the pilots. We tried to keep rat races going on all the time over the field, and I believe we all benefited from the experience. Ralph Parr was a superior adversary, as were several others, but Boots was the most fun of all. We would tangle and go all over the sky until we ran out of fuel and had to go home. I would guess we were about even-steven at the time because we were both new to the aircraft.

"When the F-86 got into a turning circle, even with full power, it began to decelerate, and the right wing had a tendency to stall, causing the aircraft to flatten in the turn. I remember going round and round with Boots with both of us losing altitude and I could look directly across the turning circle to see him looking directly across at me with neither of us gaining. It was sort of like a mutual spin with our noses pointed at each other. We always had to pull out when the ground came up, but it was great fun."

A few months later the Boy Colonel told me he was going to Korea for ninety days to learn about the jet air war. He recalls, "I wangled a 90-day temporary tour of duty in Korea to gain combat experience. We all thought that the war would be over any minute, but I had been in command of a bunch of pilots who had been in combat in Korea and it didn't seem right to be their leader if I didn't know how to lead. When I left, Boots asked me to try to get him back over for a tour in F-86s if I could swing it. At the time I didn't know how to do this because I was only going to be temporary."

Bud's plan was to somehow get to stay and command one of the two Sabre wings. He was leaving too soon to help me get there, but assured me that if I got into the Pacific theater, he would get me in his wing. That was enough for me and I began working on the idea of returning to Korea.

In December 1951 I asked our wing commander, Colonel Bob Werhle, if I could go back to Korea for an air-to-air tour. He recommended I see the personnel people in the Pentagon and then said, "If you want to go bad enough to fly copilot with me in a C-47 to the East Coast, I'll let you go." I told him he had himself a copilot and off we went.

When I went in to see the body swappers in the Pentagon, I told them I had already done an air-ground tour in F-51s and

F-80s and that I wanted to try the air-to-air mission. They agreed to assign me to an F-86 outfit, then sent me home to await orders. Sure enough, in February 1952, I got orders to Korea with assignment to the 4th Fighter-Interceptor Wing flying F-86s. I never forgot Colonel Werhle for his help. Sadly, he was killed while a two-star general in Vietnam, flying an RF-4 on a reconnaissance mission.

After getting things in order to go back to Korea, I said good-bye to everyone at George AFB. Dotty decided to stay with relatives in Phoenix, so we said our good-byes there. She was understandably unhappy about me going back to Korea, being five months pregnant, and suggested I better get this out of my system. It wasn't a model going-away scene, but I never once thought I was doing the wrong thing.

I talked to Christine only briefly. When she told me to take care of myself, she kissed me and we hugged a lot longer than necessary. Then she turned around and left.

The airplane out of Phoenix to Sacramento, which was my Stateside departure point, had been canceled. The next one out would get there via George! I have to admit I thought of the possibility of seeing Christine again when I learned the airplane was going to stay overnight at George. That afternoon, I went over to Christine's house and found a note on the door which said, "Just in case—I'm at the officers' club playing bridge." I went over, had her paged, and there she was, asking if I'd seen her note. Kind of dumbfounded, I replied, "Was that note for me?" No hesitation . . . "Yes, it was. I don't know what came over me, but I had a feeling you hadn't left for the last time. I couldn't get over that feeling, so when I came over to play bridge, I left the note on the door."

Christine left the bridge game and, divorcing herself from the implications of what was occurring, she placed herself in my hands. We got in her car, drove to San Bernardino, had dinner, went dancing, and returned. We just plain enjoyed each other's company the last few hours I was at George. One long kiss good-bye and I was gone. All during my second tour in Korea, I would hear from her but I had a difficult time writing back. Occasionally, I'd send a message or little gift to Christine and her husband, but, in general, I had little contact with her other than the letters she wrote.

CHAPTER 9

MiG Alley

When I returned to Korea in March 1952, Kimpo Air Base looked better, and why not? It had been rebuilt since I saw it last! Antiaircraft positions around the base gave me a warm feeling.

I reported in and was assigned to the 334th Fighter Squadron, 4th Fighter Wing. I moved into the room of Major George A. Davis, who had been shot down and killed in February. Those were big shoes to fill. Davis had been an ace in World War II and had fourteen kills in Korea—a record that stood for over a year. His loss was a tragic and unnecessary one. Lieutenant "Skosh" Littlefield, his wingman during that fateful mission, recalls it very well:

"We took off on the morning of 10 February in a group gaggle with George Davis leading the 334th Squadron. I was number four in his flight, as wingman for his element leader. Shortly before arriving at the Yalu River the element leader developed oxygen problems and George's wingman had reported cockpit pressurization problems. Therefore, George directed number three to return to base and take number two with him. I moved up and became George's wingman.

"We had broken away from the rest of the group and began patrolling northeast and southwest along the south side of the Yalu. As I recall, we were at around 38,000 feet. As we completed a right turn and began heading northeast, George spotted three flights of MiGs heading south across the river, well below us. They were in a close fingertip formation, flights in trail with twelve MiGs total.

"We came down on them and made our pass from their right rear and high. George opened fire on the number-four man in the last flight. I saw the MiG start smoking and fall out of formation. George then pulled out to the right, pulled up high, deployed his speed brakes, reversed his turn, and started back in for another pass. He asked me if I saw the one go down and I confirmed that I had. This all took place at about 28,000 to 30,000 feet.

"By the time we were coming in for our second pass, we had overshot the last two flights and were lined up on the lead flight. That left seven MiGs at our rear. George again selected the fourth man and began firing. By now the MiGs behind us were firing. I saw George's target start smoking and fall from the formation but almost simultaneously George's aircraft began smoking. The gear came down and I thought I heard a mike button depress and what appeared to be an attempted transmission. I have always thought that was George trying to say something, but it never came out.

"His aircraft then rolled over, did a split-S, and headed toward the ground, obviously out of control. I stayed with the aircraft through its falling-leaf-type maneuvers, called to him several times but got no response. In the meantime, several MiGs had departed formation and were chasing us. I noted several bursts of fire from them, but my greatest concentration was trying to keep George's aircraft in sight and staying with it.

"At one point a MiG crossed directly in front of me and I took a quick snapshot at him and thought I saw some hits, but my gun camera film disclosed nothing. As you may imagine, I was pretty excited about this time, as it was early in my combat career as a brand-new second lieutenant. Anyway, I continued following George and by this time I was getting radio calls from Colonel Ben Preston, who was the group leader on the mission. I confirmed that George had been hit and was going down. I gave my location and expressed my intent to stay with him as long as possible. Colonel Preston proceeded to our area to attempt a rendezvous, but never succeeded. As the aircraft approached the ground, it had assumed a nearly-wings-level diving attitude and smashed into the side of a small knoll.''

There were lessons to be learned from George Davis's loss, and I was determined not to make the same mistakes. No doubt some would think I was nuts to return to combat. Not many people went back to Korea voluntarily, and those who did had different motives. In my case, I had dreams of becoming an ace as long as I could remember. As a kid I grew up reading *G-8 and his Battle Aces* and *Tailspin Tommy* in the funny papers, dreaming of the fighter pilot's life. ''Captain Eddie'' was my hero, now joined by World War II aces like Gabreski, Mahurin, Bong, McGuire, Thyng, and others. The picture was always in the back of my mind—fighter pilots diving, climbing, turning, finally destroying the enemy aircraft; bringing honor and glory to themselves and their country. Sounds silly when you try to put it into words, but to me it was a lifelong ambition.

Professionally, I had an air-to-ground tour, was Regular Air Force intending to give it thirty years, and if I was going to go the distance, I determined to try to be better than anyone else. The way to do that was to have more experience, and returning to combat was the answer. Another influence came from the many friends I had flown with. To be frank, many of them weren't very good and they were coming back from Korea with kills. I thought to myself, ''If they can do it, I can do it, but I'll never really know till I get off my butt and get over there. No guts, no glory, babe; if you're going to do any good, you have to get in there amongst 'em.''

Most important, the thing which drove me the hardest, was my determination not to live in a world of ''ifs.'' I didn't want to go through the rest of my life saying, "If I had wanted to go back over there, I could have shot down a bunch of aircraft, too." It seemed to me that you had to decide if the objective was worth the risk, and if so, forget the rest, go for it, and take your chances. Nobody's telling you it's just as safe and easy as sitting in a rocking chair back home. You pay your money and take your chances. If you know what you're doing, and don't play the odds too close, the chances are pretty good you'll come out with something worthwhile. When I saw that line of combat-ready F-86s, I knew I had made the right decision.

I was made maintenance officer of the 334th Squadron. Colonel Mahurin told me they were going to make some changes in the squadron and that I wouldn't be there long. The 334th was changing personalities—for good or bad. Before that time came, however, there was some teeth-pulling to do. It was awful.

In the squadron, there seemed to be no firm idea of how to do things, no tactics manual with a firm set of combat guidelines. Here was a whole bunch of pseudo-experts, some of whom really didn't know what they were telling you, and didn't have enough experience to be classified as inexperienced. As a maintenance officer, new on the block, I didn't say anything about the situation, but I flew with them and watched the miserable results, promising myself that if I ever got a chance, I would change all this. Believe me, there were some great pilots in that outfit, but they needed leadership and I was in a mood to provide it.

On my second combat sortie, flying number two in Colonel Mahurin's flight, I saw my first enemy aircraft. Bud remembers it this way: "I can't forget the first time Boots saw a MiG-15. We were meeting them quite frequently at the time, but they usually stayed away from us even though we were greatly outnumbered. On this mission we spotted MiGs and gave chase, only to have them turn back and run full speed for the Manchurian border and sanctuary. Naturally, we gave chase. The MiG was a little slower than an F-86, so given enough time we could catch them, but in this case, the border kept looming up. Boots was on my right wing and as we drew closer called, 'Colonel, I'm going to get me a MiG.'' I replied, telling him to hold off for a moment longer. He repeated, 'Colonel, I'm going to get me a MiG.' With that he opened fire from very long range. Of course the F-86 immediately slowed down and there went the MiG he was chasing. Boots was really dejected when we got back to base, but it was a good lesson for us all. It was obvious that it was necessary to get right up the tail pipe before firing, because firing those six .50 caliber guns knocked off two or three knots of airspeed.''

I didn't see another MiG until my forty-eighth mission. I went to Korea expecting everyone to be a tiger and a leader, but I quickly learned that wasn't the case. When you flew, you could tell who the pussycats were.

As usual, Colonel Mahurin was right. By the time I had fifteen to twenty missions, the changes he told me about began to take place. The squadron commander went home, the operations officer got fired, and I was brought over from maintenance to be the new ops officer. These changes were made because the Boy Colonel wasn't too happy with the 334th performance. He felt, in his words, ''The 334th was not a heavy-hitting squadron at the time. Although they had spotless readiness rooms and well-kept areas, they had not destroyed many MiGs. We found the raunchy squadrons seemed to get into the most action while the 334th seemed to hold off. (Twenty-two kills in the three months before Davis's death, and only four kills in three months after). Boots was frustrated with this, but I knew it would just be a question of time before he got into a command position and would be able to change all that around.''

Mahurin met with the new 334th CO, Major Dick Ayersman, and me. ''I want to see some changes in the 334th. The name of the game is MiGs! If you two guys can't get results, we'll get a crew that can.''

On the way back to our ops building, Ayersman turned to me and said, "Since you are the new ops officer, you have until tomorrow night to come up with a plan." I already had a plan, devised from watching our pathetic performances in the air, but was he going to let me do what I felt had to be done?

The next night Dick and I got together and I laid it on the line. "If MiGs are really the name of the game, you're the one who has to go to the group commander and tell him we have to reorganize and retrain. We need at least seven days off the combat schedule to do it." He cut me off, making it clear I was asking too much, but I was heard out and before long had him convinced. Dick went to bat at group and Colonel Mahurin consented with this warning: "If that's what you need, I'll give you this opportunity, but it had better produce something." Much to our sorrow, Bud Mahurin was not to see the fruits of our labors. After racking up 3.5 kills, he was shot down by ground fire on 13 May 1952 and became a POW of the North Koreans. The tortuous struggle he went through until he was released in September 1953 has been skillfully told in his book, *Honest John*. It's a must for reading!

We began making changes—a lot of changes! The first was to ground the squadron and set aside twenty-four training sorties a day in six flights of four. Initially, I flew with each flight commander to standardize basics. The big thing I strenuously objected to was how far apart they flew—wingmen were so far away from their leaders I couldn't tell if they were MiGs or Sabres. Leaders couldn't maneuver and keep their wingmen in position. Though I was determined this was going to be the first change, I had to make the others realize the need for it.

I went to the A Flight commander, didn't brief him or anything, just told him we were going to fly formation and for him to maintain proper position. We got airborne and he was so far out there I could hardly recognize him. I racked my '86 around into him, pulling 4 or 5 Gs, and he tried to stay with me, the airplane shuddering on the edge of a high-speed stall. As he crossed my flight path, I threw out the speed brakes, rolled over the top behind him, and sat in there at his six o'clock position to embarrass him a little before pulling off to the side. I radioed, "Check six, Tom!" When I called for a rejoin, there was silence as he moved back into the same position, though not as far out. I did the same thing to him again. This guy was supposed to be a flight commander and he was embarrassed!

The third time he was so close he could read the numbers on my tail, and that's exactly where I wanted him. I didn't turn quite as tight, and since he stayed with me, we graduated to loops, rolls, aerobatics, turn reversals in formation—everything went great. He was a good pilot, just didn't know where he should be to stay with a maneuvering leader.

Back in the briefing room I said, "That was a pretty good flight, Tom, but what happened? You had such a good position when we first got up there. Why were you flying so close to me at the end?" He shot back, "My God, you didn't expect me to stay with you in those maneuvers. I had to get closer to keep from losing you!" With a grin I said, "You just passed the test. I'll give you eight sorties per day and you teach that lesson to each pilot in your flight. There'll be other things I'll demand of you, but for now don't come back until you've got wingmen who can stick with you while you're pulling Gs and turning."

I repeated this with all four flight commanders, and two did fine. I transferred the other two—they would never make it. I recall telling one, "I'm sorry as hell, but you've been here sixty-five missions without a fight. You either don't want to fight or are the unluckiest guy I've ever known. Either way, I can't afford you." It is difficult to tell the difference sometimes between bad luck and no guts. You don't win popularity contests making decisions like that, but guys risking their lives deserve the best leadership possible. Those two had to go!

One new leader I appointed was a sharp, enterprising first

lieutenant named Charles "Chick" Cleveland. He really could fly the airplane, and though he wasn't the ranking officer, he deserved the position and he got it. Chick, who eventually became a three-star general, remembers the reorganization period this way:

"Major Blesse was a hell of a force in our squadron. He and I got to Kimpo about the same time in early 1952, I as a green lieutenant and he as a seasoned captain who already had flown a tour in F-51s and F-80s. It was clear that Boots was not there simply because he had to be or because it was the thing to do. He was there with a purpose, to accomplish something, to contribute and to excel. And he did all the above.

"After some time in the maintenance business, Boots became the operations officer and took it on himself to reshape the flying part of the squadron in his own image. With his previous tour, he had a lot of credibility with the pilots, especially with us younger guys. He was convinced the squadron had not been aggressive enough, was using questionable tactics, and had generally not been well led at the flight level. He took the unprecedented step of standing us down from the combat schedule, relieving some flight commanders and appointing new ones, and initiating an intensive training program that had us all breathing hard and looking forward to getting back into the sky over North Korea. And Manchuria.

"Our morale went up along with the kill ratio, and Boots himself set a great example of personal combat leadership. 'No guts, no glory, men,' he would tell us with almost gleeful enthusiasm. He was aggressive but not foolhardy, had great hands and instincts, and was impatient with those who didn't meet his own high standards of commitment and excellence.

"Boots was a tireless worker on the ground. Among other things he did well, he played a mean game of Ping-Pong. I was the squadron athletic officer and had built and painted a pretty good facsimile of a Ping-Pong table for the ready room. I could beat anybody in the squadron except Boots, and he took great pleasure in whipping me in front of the other pilots. If I was reading or drinking coffee when he marched in, I knew what was coming. He would pick up a paddle and ask with a smirk, 'How's your Ping-Pong today, lieutenant?' It was good but not good enough, and I thought I knew how those ten enemy pilots felt when Boots got behind them. It was kill or be killed.

"Boots was ambitious but not overly so. I flew his wing several times when I was a buck pilot, and after he made me a flight commander, he took me up on a MiG-hunting expedition to the Yalu and well beyond. At the time, I had four confirmed kills and he had eight or nine. We searched high and low for MiGs, and when we saw two aircraft below the horizon way out, in a most unselfish gesture he gave me the lead and said, 'Go get 'em.'

"We dived to the attack but they turned out to be '86s, so I broke off and Boots took the lead again. We kept looking, getting lower and lower on fuel, and since I had to jockey the throttle to stay in good position, I had less fuel than he did. He tried to keep track of my fuel state but I didn't want to worry him unnecessarily. Finally, when I was down to 1,300 pounds and we were about thirty miles north of Antung, I said, 'Gotta go home.'

"Boots gave me the lead again, and I zoom-climbed to about 50,000 feet. About a hundred miles from base I stop-cocked the throttle with less than 500 pounds left and set up optimum glide speed for home. Boots flew wing at idle power, gave me cover, gave me encouragement, and gave me directions, as my canopy had iced over. When we reached 2,000 feet I could see again, and there was Kimpo dead ahead. I had enough fuel to restart the engine, enter initial, and make a normal pattern and landing. Ho hum, another day at the office with Boots!

"Boots was an articulate, thoughtful, dedicated guy who made half a career out of the *No Guts, No Glory* business, which evolved into an Air Force Fighter Weapons School manual on fighter tactics. For me, at an impressionable time in my career, he also served as a role model for personal excellence and strong leadership. He showed us that one man can make a difference. The experience helped make me a better officer and stood me in good stead my entire career.''

After the flight commanders had been thoroughly briefed on the entire program, they began training their own people. Then I set up a few new rules of engagement.

It was an absolute no-no to get into a fight with MiGs and have the leader and wingman get separated. That's how you lose people. With high-speed airplanes all over the sky, if you didn't stick together you could lose a wingman in a matter of seconds. I made a hard and fast rule—any wingman that lost contact with his leader in combat was grounded for a week with a chore of extra duty. We'd assign an average pilot to fly with him and put him up for formation flying in the local area, which really chapped him. When he got back, he was a different man. Actually, that only happened about twice and we never had any more trouble.

We also established new squadron procedures. The previous operations officer would sit all afternoon in the ops room and struggle with the schedule. I didn't want anything to do with that—I felt the flight commander should choose his men. I called in the four flight commanders and said, "You guys are king. Every one of you have a certain number of people under your control; they belong to you. I'm not going to censure one of them, the squadron commander isn't going to censure one of them, but if one is out of line, we'll come after you. Better be sure whatever they're doing is right.'' We made them live, eat, and fly together, then I had the flight commanders put up a training board with all their pilots' names on it. Each had to get at least three dogfights a week in order to be qualified to fly a mission. We had people fly a hundred missions and never see an enemy airplane, then rotate home. When I'd run into them back in the States, they were tactics experts! It was a disgrace.

Pilots simply did not have the opportunity to meet the enemy often enough, including me, and nobody looked harder than I did. When I went on my eighty-eighth mission, I had only two kills and five sightings. I was keeping charts in a little book. When I had a sighting, I'd log it with the results. It averaged out to a kill about every third sighting. All kinds of things would happen: a tank wouldn't feed or you couldn't drop it; you would be heading home and sight a MiG but not have enough fuel to engage him. A million things could happen that prevented you from taking advantage of a sighting. I made it a rule to debrief all sightings at a squadron meeting. We knew we'd make mistakes, but the object was not to repeat them. The point was to learn from each other's experience and get better.

The bottom line of all this was maintaining pilot proficiency in spite of little actual combat. No good golf pro would enter a tournament when he hadn't played in two weeks. Those guys practice all the time, hitting five hundred balls or more a day, and they only play for money while a fighter pilot plays for his life. Day after day, we'd go up and back, up and back, into MiG Alley without getting into a fight. Then, bang, after ten or fifteen missions, there's a really donnybrook and half the '86s would get spread to the winds. I hoped to prevent that by requiring each pilot to have three dogfights a week. "If you've gotten into a fight with a MiG, that counts as one. If you haven't gotten three fights this week and your week is coming to an end, the flight leader must come back a little early, get off to the side of the field and have a real good fight between the two elements, then come on in and land. That way everyone gets some practice. Log the fight on your flight chart so I can see the status of training at all times."

Many complained that they didn't see the value of my plan, thinking it was kid stuff, but I watched the skill level go up and it did them more good than they knew.

At the end of our week out of combat, we were back in business, but it was up and back, up and back, and no MiGs. This was really cruel after going through so much retraining, getting the guys ready. We needed something to happen, particularly since there were so many doubters about the value of reorganization. I'd guess many of those guys thought I had a big hole in my head, particularly since I didn't have a single kill at the time. I needed something to happen and it did.

Fortunately for me, I downed my first MiG on 25 May 1952. This was the greatest thing that could have happened to me, not for my sake, but because all the principles we'd been talking about were proven. That day we got in a big fight, my wingman stayed with me, everything worked like it was supposed to, we shot down an airplane, and came home intact as a team. On debriefing, we went through it and found everyone had done the right thing. It had a very positive effect on the outfit—and had some effects on me that were a little surprising.

My first aerial victory pumped a combination of anxiety, thrill, eagerness, and maybe even a little fear into me. We spotted two MiGs, higher than we were, that obviously didn't see us. About 25,000 feet, the MiG-15 had double the F-86's rate of climb and was a little faster, so I tried to cut to the inside and gradually gain on them. All of a sudden the lead MiG's wing dropped, the nose came around, and I could feel the hair at the base of my neck try to stand up. I realized there, in that moment of time, I saw him, he saw me, and one of us was not going home. The world's most dangerous game had begun.

I was anxious, eager, excited, and scared all at once. I'd come all this way to do this single thing, yet I wasn't sure I was prepared. How good was the MiG-15? All I knew was what I had been told. Now I was about to find out for myself. We closed rapidly, me climbing and the MiG turning and diving slightly. We passed within a few hundred yards—our combined speeds about 1,000 mph. For some reason, he continued to try to turn into me, and since I was slower, it was easy to outturn him. At that moment he could have straightened out, continued diving and quickly been out of gun range. Instead, he made a very bad decision and tried to reverse. I slid in behind him and began shooting into that MiG-15, but nothing happened. No pieces, no fire, no bailout—nothing! He was accelerating away from me and in a second or two was out of gun range and climbing for the Yalu. I followed underneath, watching him get away. I couldn't believe this was happening. Smoke began coming from his engine, so I continued following him with one eye on my fuel gauge. He seemed to be maintaining his airspeed, and the gauge said start home *now*, so reluctantly I began a turn to the south.

I was crushed! So close and nothing! One last look and the MiG was still trailing smoke. I began the painful duty of transferring my thoughts to the business of getting home. Suddenly my wingman shouted, "There he goes, Red Lead, he punched out." I whirled around in time to see the smoking MiG in a deep descending spiral and a beautiful white parachute. That MiG pilot made two or three really dumb decisions in our brief encounter. As a result, my first fight left me confident, elated, and a little shaky.

Sitting in the debriefing, as the intelligence officer queried me, I was embarrassed. He asked question after question I couldn't answer. I was too excited. I didn't know if it was a right or left turn, though I remembered it had started at 32,000 feet. After about fifteen blanks to his eager questions, he blurted out, "Say, you were there, weren't you?"

That made me mad . . . "Yeah, you're damn right and let me tell you something, I was there, I saw his airplane smoke, and I saw the bugger bail out. That's all you need to know, and I'll talk to you after my next kill." Then I walked out.

Almost a month later, on 20 June, I got another kill, a prop-driven LA-9. There were sixteen Sabres trying to knock down two World War II type fighters by coming in very, very fast, taking a couple of quick shots, then chandelling up another 5,000 feet to await the next turn. One Lavochkin pilot was playing them like a piano, knowing exactly what each '86 was going to do. Just before each Sabre was within firing range, the LA-9 would go into a tight little turn. The '86 pilot would shoot a couple of wild bursts and chandelle back up.

I was at 18,000 feet when I first saw them. When I noticed a break in the cycle, I said a little silent prayer . . . "If one more guy misses, he's all mine." It was P-51s at George all over again. I radioed my wingman, "We're going to be too low—stay with three and check my six." While they orbited, giving me a little cover, I peeled off. Down almost in the weeds, I watched the '86 in front chandelle out, popped my speed brakes, pulled the throttle all the way back to idle, and started coming up at him. He saw me and put the Lavochkin into that real tight turn, but I just kept going up. He rolled out, just like he'd been doing, thinking he was perfectly safe. I rolled over, came up about 400 feet behind him, gaining on him. It would have been better to be about 1,500 feet back gaining the way I was, but you can't always get what you want in air combat.

Firing on him, I didn't want to overshoot. He would have been very dangerous since he had better maneuvering performance, better turn capability, and better everything except acceleration. Even that wasn't good insurance—by the time I could get any acceleration from my jet, he'd have taught me an unforgettable lesson. As I slid up on him there were several hits, then the LA-9 blew up with me about 200 feet underneath. Oil covered my canopy like someone had pulled a shade over it. I couldn't see anything, and I knew I was overtaking him. This was too close for comfort. Looking out over the back of the canopy, trying to fly the airplane, I was hoping that was the end of him. For all I knew, I could have hit the oil tank and he could still have time to fire at me before the engine froze up.

I took as big a turn as I could get, pulled in the speed brakes, and gave it all the throttle I had. At about 350 knots the air started blowing the oil back—the shade came up and I could see again. The LA-9 went into a steep turn and crashed. The whole exercise went against everything we'd been taught. Unless you knew exactly what you were doing, slowing down in combat was very dangerous. In this case, since I had fought P-51s so much at George, I felt I was justified in getting the LA-9. Dozens of times, flailing around with the Mustangs, I had screwed it up. But I learned. I knew well the consequences of getting it wrong and felt there was acceptable risk for me if I went about it properly. That's one of the reasons I wanted my wingman to stay out of the fight—I didn't want to be in a firing position and see him go by with the throttle off, speed brakes out, feet sticking out, sailing right in front of the LA-9. In some books, it was dumb. In my book, it was a calculated risk which I reasoned was worth taking. At best it was a fine line between something dumb and an act that characterized you as an outstanding pilot.

Later, after three or four victories, I was surprised at how cold and calculating I had become. At times, I almost felt ashamed. I never thought I'd get that way, but, to be honest, I never wanted it any different. I could come back with every single detail: altitudes, maneuvers, sun position, clouds, everything! Better still, it wasn't instinct flying. I was thinking my way through each fight. The one thing that never left me was the intense, gripping anxiety and excitement that occurred when I saw some kind of movement that indicated the enemy had seen me and one of us wasn't going home. That remained and has to this day been the greatest thrill of my life.

Seeing MiGs so seldom, sometimes I was too aggressive. During one mission, we spotted MiGs and dropped external fuel tanks to prepare to fight. I had one tank that wouldn't jettison. This slowed the airplane down quite a bit and made it stall in some pretty funny attitudes. The MiGs were below us and we hadn't seen any for some time, a combination that was hard to avoid for a hungry fighter pilot. Just one pass . . . that's all I'd need. With my wingman I began my single pass, but suddenly we were attacked by two MiGs we didn't see. The next five minutes almost ended my combat tour. My wingman had released both of his tanks—no need to get him shot down just because I couldn't maneuver very well. I told him I'd be okay, gave him a heading home, and a terse order to get the hell out of there. My words were still echoing in my mike when I got the first burst of MiG fire. "Jesus, that was close."

The MiG-15 had two 23mm guns and one 37mm cannon. When the cannon was fired, you could actually see the rounds coming and going. He shot slightly under me, maybe six or eight feet, and I got the unmistakable feeling it was time to do something—anything! I rolled that '86 over and headed down, pulling as many Gs as I could. With that external tank still hung up, anything I could do, he could do better. By the time I got to the deck, I had been fired at twice more. The thought struck me that I had a North Korean Mahurin on my ass.

By now we were as close to the ground as I could get. I headed right at anything that stuck up above the ground, turning at the last second, hoping he would run into it. We were approaching Antung, a large city on the north side of the Yalu River. Buildings, towers—any structure became an aiming point. The two of us went through the middle of town like a cyclone; turning, climbing, diving to street level again, narrowly missing every building, provided I kept going south. The MiG driver was determined to keep me from getting away. He knew he had me if he just played it right.

Suddenly, it was over. South of Antung we headed out over the water, and his directives said no to that. I never saw him turn away. I kept checking six, inverting my aircraft to be sure he wasn't underneath me, and never saw him again. We controlled the sea; if he went down over water, he was a prisoner. If we splashed, we got a free ride home. I climbed out and headed for home.

Climbing through that peaceful blue sky, I remember muttering into my oxygen mask, "Blesse, you dumb bastard, if you ever try anything like that again, you deserve to get wired." I never did. That night, I went to the club and celebrated the arrival of my brand-new daughter, Melanie Diane Blesse, born 25 June 1952.

All the pilots that were getting any kills suffered from over-aggressiveness now and then. Captain Bob Straub was a good example. We were forbidden to cross the Yalu River but we did it anyway; we had to if we were going to protect the fighter-bombers. One rule specifically ordered us not to strafe MiGs on their airfields, all of which were across the river—an absolute no-no. If he was flying, okay, shoot him down, but if he was even rolling down the runway, no dice, because that's really ground attack. That's a new ball game.

This was just too much one day for Bob Straub. Seeing some MiGs go back across the Yalu, he followed until he caught up with them strung out and entering the pattern for landing. Coming down from 15,000 feet, Straub could see the last guy getting ready to land. He wasn't about to let that MiG get away, so he rolled over and came down like greased lightning. Screaming in at a million mph, Straub saw the MiG put down gear and flaps, and realized he was going way too fast. Speed brakes out, throttle chopped to idle, Straub overshot on the MiG's crosswind leg. Bob zoomed up, turned around, pushed down, and overshot him on the downwind leg also.

As the MiG made its turn onto base, Straub again had to pull up to kill his speed. Just about the time Straub got into position on base leg, the MiG turned onto final. Our boy turned with him until both were 300 yards apart on final approach to this air base in Manchuria, forbidden territory. Straub started thinking about the rules—can't hit him if he's on the ground—and he'd worked so doggone hard to get this far. Just as he was about to open fire he saw the nose of the MiG coming up, flaring for touchdown. As the tires squeaked onto the runway, there was a long silence on the radio, then I heard Straub's voice, "Bounce, you son of a bitch, and you've had it!"

From May through September 1952, the Chinese Air Force tried to wrest air superiority over North Korea from the United

Nations by bringing in more MiGs. The first step was building more bases in Manchuria, then in North Korea. During this time they kept negotiating for peace at Panmunjom, but before a treaty was signed, they wanted those airfields in place. At the very last minute they could fly a couple hundred airplanes into North Korea and have a full-sized air force ready to go after the signing.

One spring afternoon, flying over Manchuria where I shouldn't have been, I noticed some markings near a little place called Fen Chen that looked like a new runway. After getting back to base, I grabbed an intelligence officer I knew fairly well, swore him to secrecy, and told him what I saw. He asked me to keep an eye on it, so once a week I'd slip into Manchuria to see what had been accomplished. Over the next month or so, I watched that place grow from a few scratches in the ground to a 6,000-foot cement runway complete with pre-fab buildings and airplanes being worked on—MiGs. This was happening in three other places that I could see, so by the time May rolled around, they had the capability of launching 600 or 700 MiGs. We had from 150 to 225 F-86s in the entire theater to oppose them, and many of those were out of commission for lack of parts and various other reasons.

Just before a large attack on targets in the northernmost part of Korea, Colonel Mahurin called four of us in for a private meeting. He didn't swear us to secrecy or anything like that, but he made it clear this was something we didn't talk about, and that it was strictly voluntary.

"We have a big mission tomorrow with three groups of fighter-bombers going up north. They'll face four hundred MiGs coming off those fields if we can't keep them on the ground. I know you all have friends in the fighter-bomber units. What's your pleasure?" Four hands went up. He continued, "I wish I could give you guys twenty-four airplanes apiece, but I can only set aside four per enemy base." We were each assigned a MiG field—I got Fen Chen.

"You can't strafe them on the ground, but do whatever you

can to keep those airplanes on the ground for eighteen minutes—that's all you'll need to get the fighter-bomber boys in and out and on their way home.''

Having watched Fen Chen from the word go, I took my flight in and arrived about twenty minutes before the strike was to begin. The Chinese would be tracking them on radar before they arrived at their targets. I could tell when our guys were reasonably close to their target, because the MiGs started rolling out. Before long there must have been forty or fifty of them taxiing all at one time, nose to tail! We circled the base at about 18,000 feet and watched until the first two airplanes started their run-up for takeoff. It was easy to tell because of all the debris blowing away behind them. That was the cue for me to take my wingman and start down on them. I could see them start their takeoff roll and initially I thought I was too late. Someone in the tower, however, was on my side and told them they had F-86s on final. I could see the blue smoke from their tires as they applied brakes in a panic, but they were in that no-man's-land without enough room to stop. That leader and wingman went right off the end of the runway, then past the field boundary, breaking off both nose gears. What a beautiful sight! Two tail pipes sticking up in the air about a hundred feet off the end of the runway.

We pulled up to 15,000 feet without firing a shot and started orbiting again. I couldn't believe my eyes! The MiGs started taxiing back on another taxiway. In about twenty minutes, all the fighter-bombers had come and gone and we'd pulled it off. It was with some measure of satisfaction that we realized when Sabres were in the area, the MiGs would never take off and challenge us. That was important to know.

Nothing big happened for two or three weeks, then the big payoff came on 6 August. Someone must have called into the MiG operations room with orders from the Party Chairman—''You buggers have got to fly and this is the day we're going to seize air superiority from the bloody Yankees!''

When we approached MiG Alley, basically northwestern

North Korea, it was wall-to-wall MiG-15s. Everywhere you turned, there was a flight to deal with. My squadron got in a big melee, coming out the other side with three kills, a probable, two damaged, and not a single wingman lost. Though I got one of the kills (my third), this was overshadowed by the electrifying effect the fight had on the outfit. There were no more doubting Thomases. All we had since the reorganization was a few guys getting sporadic kills, but on 6 August it was teamwork and tactics that carried the day. It was obvious even to those of little faith that what we had done for the 334th made the squadron a successful fighting unit.

There had been only two flights scheduled that day, one to the north sector of MiG Alley and one to the south. The other flight leader was Lieutenant Chick Cleveland, whom I had promoted to command beyond his rank. Chick and I flipped a coin to see who got which one. He went north and I took the south. When we got back, it was easy to tell who had fired and who hadn't by looking at the black powder smudges around the gun ports. When I saw Chick's airplane coming in with no smudges, I got on the radio and said, "How about going over to D channel?" He switched so we could talk without bothering anybody. I told him there were MiGs everywhere. "How'd you do?" After a long silence, I heard loud and clear in a disgusted tone, "If they sawed a woman in two, I'd get the half that eats." Chick was our youngest flight commander, an outstanding pilot who distinguished himself in every possible way. He got four kills along with several probables and a couple damaged. He was made an honorary member of the American Fighter Aces Association ("The Ivory Ace," 99 44/100ths percent pure) and retired a three-star general.

While the other squadrons got about one or two apiece and had a few flights separated, we came home together and had more victories. After that, everybody in the outfit practiced without being told. At last they could see that it worked. During that month our squadron got eleven kills, with another seventeen in September. Our tactics changes had paid off handsomely. For a while at least, we ruled the roost!

After my fourth kill on 20 August, plus a probable and three damaged, I was coming up on ninety-five missions and rotation. I wanted that fifth kill so bad I could taste it. The group commander, Colonel Royal Baker, came around every evening, telling me I ought to go home. I had done my duty. I owed it to my family to come home. Other aces had warned me about Baker; he was really too immature to be a good group commander. He felt as though we were in competition with him, not working for him. He was a one-man board of inquiry every time someone came back with a kill. I finally told him it took me my whole lifetime to get where I was and that I not only didn't want to go home, I wanted to extend for twenty-five more missions. He finally left me alone and directed his campaign against one of the other aces.

Korea made you feel lousy; tired of the huts, roaches, uncomfortable bunks, poor food, and no women. But it was the only place you could get this kind of experience. I put in for another twenty-five missions and it was approved.

I had been caught up in the Ace syndrome long before I got to Korea, so wanting that fifth kill was not new to me, though it was to quite a few other guys. Many would get close and wrestle with the problem of whether to go home or extend for twenty-five more missions, hoping to get that last MiG.

One pilot got to ninety-four missions with four kills. He had been writing his wife for weeks telling her when he was going to be back and suddenly he got in the middle of several fights, coming back every day with a MiG. Then, at ninety-five missions, he *had* to extend. He decided to send her a telegram, which read, "Dear Joyce, I'm at 95 missions. I have four MiGs, must get fifth MiG to become ace. Have decided to extend 25 missions. Be home in about two months. [signed] Joe." He thought that ought to do it—surely she'd understand how important this thing was to him.

About four days later a telegram arrived for Joe. Opening it up, he read, "Dear aspiring ace: I, too, have made an important decision. I am going to have a baby in nine months and seven days, and if you want to be in on it, you better get home!" Joe never made ace!

Flying my 104th mission on 4 September 1952, I got my fifth victory. Earl Brown ("Brownie," I called him) was my wingman and had been with me during at least one other successful flight. I liked Brownie. He was a fine pilot, cool under pressure, knew his job to the nth degree, and had a good sense of humor. We all used to kid about having sweaty palms, which we thought was an indication the MiGs would be flying that day. I'd often rub Brownie's short haircut, telling him what good luck he brought me. I rubbed it on 4 September 1952.

We had made a couple of passes through MiG Alley with no contact. Suddenly I spotted two '15s about eleven o'clock high. "Padlock," I called to Brownie. That meant I had my eyes on enemy aircraft and that from here on he was responsible to check six for us both. "Roger," Brownie countered.

We dropped our external tanks and began increasing speed as we cut to the inside of a very lazy turn the MiGs were making. "You're clear," Brownie barked. Suddenly the leader began a sharp turn into us and the hair prickled a little on the back of my neck. One of us wasn't going home. As he turned toward us, I pulled up steeply and rolled over, following him around the turn and through the dive that followed. "You're clear," Brownie assured me once again. The MiG leader's wingman was thrown off in a reversal, and headed for the Yalu River and safety.

In the next turn, I was in range for a shot and lit up his fuselage and right wing with my .50 calibers. Suddenly it was over—he ejected! It all happened so fast it took me a moment to two to realize I had just gotten number five. Before I could even think Ace, the words "You're clear" jolted me back to reality. Old Brownie was out there doing his job and saving my ass from being picked off while I thought of the wrong things. As usual, fuel was low and it was more than time to get out of there. I thought of a hundred good things about Brownie right then, but all I said was, "Okay, Brownie, I got it. Let's go home!" It was no accident he got three stars before he retired.

As we climbed out, I thought of all the enemy territory we had to fly over to get home. In the back of my mind a little prayer began popping out. "Lord, if you have to take me while I'm over here, don't do it today. Let me get back and tell someone I finally got number five." It was the realization of a dream that I had since I was a kid, and over the years it came to mean more to me even than becoming a general officer in the Air Force.

Up to this point I had earned a few Air Medals and Distinguished Flying Crosses for my two Korean tours. In the past, in Korea, when one became an ace it was customary to get a Silver Star, so the 5th Air Force commander, Lieutenant General Glenn O. Barcus, came down personally to present it to me. George Davis was killed in action after fourteen kills, so Gabby Gabreski, the USAF's top living ace, was leading the active Korean aces with 6.5 kills. In the 4th Group, Harry Thyng and Cliff Jolley both had five.

During my 107th mission on 8 September, I jumped a flight of twelve with just my wingman, and I recall radioing to him, "If these guys have read Chapter Two, we're not going to be here very long." We pressed on into the rear flight, which turned off. I watched to see if they were going to turn back, but they just kept going.

We flew up fairly close to the second flight and they broke off, and I was again watching to see if they'd come back, but they kept going as well. Now we were down to two on four, which isn't too bad. Suddenly the second element broke off and I was sure these guys would turn into us. Nope, they went off like the others, so we attacked the two-ship flight. The wingman broke away. I shot the leader down after a half loop and a couple of turns, then went after the wingman and got him also. It was getting easier.

News of the two kills brought Harry Thyng and Cliff Jolley out to greet me in the parking area. Throwing his arms around me, Colonel Thyng said, "Damn, Boots, it's about time somebody in this wing was the leading ace." He was referring to Gabby Gabreski. It was just a competitive situation, since Thyng was commander of the 4th Wing at Kimpo and Gabreski had the 51st Wing at Suwon.

On 15 and 17 September, I got the eighth and ninth red stars painted under my canopy, but in getting number nine, I almost lost my wingman. We had closed in on a MiG-15 and were getting fairly close. My wingman, to keep from getting thrown too far out in the turns, was crossing back over from outside to inside each time I made a tight turn.

On one of those crossovers, he was coming underneath just as I was firing and tearing some pretty-good-size pieces off the MiG. A big hunk of his stabilizer came off, went underneath my airplane, and got sucked into my wingman's airscoop. It just corncobbed his engine, taking off all the compressor blades, leaving him with nothing but a whirling dervish that gave no thrust. He had to shut it down and eject into the water. We got a chopper out there, picked him up and brought him home with no injuries. He was the only wingman I had who didn't come back in his own aircraft.

On 3 October 1952 for my 123d mission, two away from going home, I took a wingman who had only a few missions. There were seven or eight of us who used to get into the MiGs quite a bit, and we found if we could get a new guy in action during his first eight or ten missions, he turned out to be a pretty darned good combat pilot. On the other hand, if he went up and back, up and back, of twenty-five or thirty trips and never saw anything, he was apt to end up a little less aggressive than we wanted him to be.

We cruised around looking for MiGs, but we didn't see

anything. I mean everything was dead. Number Four developed fuel problems, so Three took him home. As we got down close to Bingo (just enough fuel to get home with a small margin of safety), we turned around and started south. We had quite a bit of enemy territory to cross before ''going feet wet'' over the water. As we leveled off at around 31,000 feet, about two hundred miles from home, I saw a flight of four MiGs at our six o'clock, out about a mile or two. We were getting fairly close to the water so I nosed over a bit to pick up speed. We didn't have the fuel to fight, so I wanted to get over the water and continue home.

I think the lead MiG pilot realized what was happening because he started firing his guns. The 23s were ineffective, but when he fired that 37 you could see it coming like a Roman candle. I had the living daylights scared out of me the first time I ''trapped'' a MiG at my six o'clock, firing away. Well, my wingman had never seen an enemy airplane, so all he saw when he looked back was big cannonballs coming at him, even though the tracers were falling far short. Without thinking, he broke away from me, which was just what the MiG leader wanted. The '15 cut to the inside of the Sabre's turn and rapidly began to close the range.

One glance at the situation and I thought, Christ, we don't have enough fuel for this. Nevertheless, I came around and radioed, ''Put it in a spiral and keep at least four Gs on it; I'm coming down.'' He got his '86 in a spiral, with the MiG leader and his wingman in a trailing spiral trying to get him, while I fell in behind them with the other element of two MiGs behind me. We had a big daisy chain winding down from 31,000. As we hit 18,000 I was getting even more concerned about fuel—there wasn't enough of it left to do anything but break for home.

The second MiG wasn't doing as well as the leader, who was gaining on my wingman. He slid out, giving me the chance to get a couple of bursts off. A couple of pieces flew off, then I got a good burst into him. He rolled out right away and must have told his leader, who probably didn't want to be there by himself, and broke off as well. Now there was just me and the two MiGs behind me. I radioed a little more advice to my wingman. "Keep that thing at .9, get it over the water, and head for home. Don't worry about me." He got out and made it back okay.

Meanwhile the third MiG started firing at me. It was easier for him since I had eased off a little to fire at the number-two man. Seeing a couple of rounds go by, I tightened my turn, reversed into him, and we crossed at a pretty high angle. I held my turn, then rolled over in a dive. As frequently happened during those damn fights, I looked around after I pulled out and found I was all by myself. I knew two MiGs were there somewhere, but I couldn't find a thing.

I stayed in a tight turn for about ten seconds, worried somebody was going to take a shot at me. Then I looked at my fuel gauge—1,100 pounds. If the winds were right, I'd make it with fumes, but if they were wrong, I'd have to try to land on the beach on Peng Yeng Do, a small island off the coast. I started climbing to save fuel. Around 11,000, I caught a glimpse of something out of the corner of my left eye—a MiG, coming down on me from ten o'clock. This is it, I thought, school's out. I don't have any fuel to fight with this guy. For some reason he never saw me, diving right in front of my '86. As he came by, I looked at my fuel gauge, looked at the MiG, and said, "Hell, it's a toss-up anyway. Why not?"

Pulling about a 4-G turn, I climbed to the right and rolled off the top underneath him. It took about twenty-five seconds—I closed to 600 feet, fired, and watched the MiG explode and begin burning, then saw the pilot eject. I rolled right back out on course, figuring it cost me about 200 pounds of fuel to shoot him down. There went number ten but I was down to 900 pounds. I hoped the camera film worked; otherwise, no confirmation.

The alert flight at Kimpo, led by Captain Robbie Risner, had been scrambled after hearing we were in a fight and short on fuel. A five-kill ace at that point, with another three MiGs to come, Robbie was one of the USAF's finest fighter pilots. About thirteen years later, he was shot down in Vietnam, spending seven years as a POW under horrible circumstances, as described in his fine book, *Passing of the Night*. It was a good thing Robbie and his flight saw the burning MiG-15 or I wouldn't have gotten credit for my last kill. I didn't think I would make it back and my film would be lost with the aircraft.

I was still over North Korea. I called Dumbo, the rescue flying boat that was always on station during our missions, and told him to orbit Peng Yeng Do Island. "If I can't make it home, that's where I'm going to try to land." If I could get a hundred miles out at 39,000 feet with 300 pounds of fuel, shutting down the engine would allow me to glide back to base at 180 knots, putting me in the traffic pattern at 6,000 feet where I could restart and land. But I only made it to about 32,000 feet when I hit 300 pounds. Without tailwinds there wasn't a chance. Calling the base, I asked what the winds were and they replied, "Out of the southwest." Nothing could have been worse. I shut the engine off and began a 180-knot glide toward Kimpo Air Base.

As I passed 17,000 feet, I decided I'd become a POW if I stayed on this course. I had no relish for that, especially after Pyongyang Sally had broadcast the night of my eighth kill, "Just wait, Major Blesse, we're going to get you, and when we do, we're going to hang you from the Han River Bridge." I changed course and continued my glide toward the west coast and the island. I called Dumbo again. "I'm probably not going to make it, so orbit between the shore and the island." He acknowledged.

I continued to glide down at 180 knots but the wind was against me. For a while I didn't think I'd even get to the coast. At about 7,000 feet everything looked like it was much too far away, so I restarted the engine and used my remaining fuel to climb as high as I could. At 13,000 the thing flamed out, so I reestablished a 180-knot glide, hoping I'd make the water. I had to cross a main supply route, and I drew a tremendous amount of enemy fire. Several times the flak bursts were so close one wing or the other would raise up. I had no choice but to be a predictable target—jinking would cost me airspeed and altitude—so I held my heading and hoped I wouldn't get "the golden BB" (a direct hit).

I finally crossed the North Korean coast at about 3,000 feet, but a half mile or so out over the water, I knew I was getting too low. Time to get out, I thought, so I called Dumbo. "I can't go any farther; I'm getting out. Don't let my aircraft hit you." Instantly he radioed back, "Rog, we've got you in sight."

Then occurred one of the finest things that ever happened to me in the Air Force, something I'll never forget. We had a radio in wing operations, and when the guys weren't flying, they all went up there to listen to what was being said in the combat area. It wasn't unusual to find fifteen or twenty pilots sitting around listening to what was happening on the mission. Chick Cleveland recalls that day well:

"I was in the operations room monitoring the squadron combat frequency on 3 October 1952 when Boots ran out of luck and fuel (but not judgment) after downing his tenth enemy aircraft. He was very calm as he headed for Chodo, an island in our hands in the East China Sea, for a planned bailout. Things were pretty tense in ops as the conversation on the radio made it apparent that our leader might not make it back.

"The special bonding that takes place between fighter pilots in combat made us feel that a part of us was up there with him. Five or six of us grabbed the mike and gave him some quick words of encouragement. All I could think to say over the radio just before his ejection was something like, 'Congratulations on number ten. We'll have a seat for you at the bar—see you when you get back.' His reply was equally original, like, 'Roger.' And out he went."

I heard it from the listening end of my radio. Right after I told Dumbo I wasn't going to make it and had to eject, I heard,

"Take it easy, Boots." Then another guy on, "See you at supper." And another, "Don't forget you owe me five bucks, so get your butt back here." One message after another from six or seven guys. I remember very clearly a chill going up and down my spine and saying, "God, what a great bunch of guys."

My hands went to the seat triggers. *Boom!* Explosive charges blew me and the seat, with parachute attached, into the slipstream. Out I went at about 1,200 feet, a little too low. I didn't want to get tied up with the seat so I undid my seatbelt before ejecting. The chute opened, pulling me away from the seat instantly. Almost immediately I went into the water. My throat burned in the saltwater from a parachute strap abrasion. One of my pockets was open and all my maps and survival gear floated out.

After inflating my one-man raft I swam over and picked up my helmet, which for some reason had not sunk. Very carefully I put everything back in the dinghy, then climbed aboard myself. Just about the time I was set for the winter, the Dumbo landed and taxied over to me.

A line was fired out an open window, which I grabbed, and I was pulled over to the airplane and inside. As soon as I was in, the pilot hit the throttles to get out of there. Scrambling to my feet, I ran up the aisle to the cockpit—and started banging on the pilot's helmet. "Wait, a minute! My dinghy is still out there with all my stuff in it!" With a quick, disgusted look at me, he said, "Fuck your dinghy. They're shooting at me and we're getting the hell out of here!" My dinghy became a target for Risner's alert flight, which sent it to the bottom of the East China Sea with my F-86.

By the time I got back to Kimpo, word of my bailout had already gone to the Pentagon and a wire had come back which read, "Subject: Major Frederick C. Blesse. Subject officer will be returned to the Z1 immediately before we have another Davis incident." This referred to George Davis's death in action the previous February. He had extended his tour voluntarily, as I had, and since he was the leading ace, the Air Force got some bad publicity when he was shot down. They didn't want it to happen again, so my tour ended abruptly though I was 2 missions short of the 125 I had volunteered for. In any event, I was now the leading ace in Korea, and though I suspected it wouldn't last too long, I intended to enjoy every minute of it. The next day I was in Japan for a series of press conferences.

CHAPTER 10

A Time for Thanks

The time in Tokyo was interesting. I had several interviews with reporters; answering questions about my combat tour, my recent bailout into the East China Sea, relative performance of the MiG-15 and the F-86, and other touchy subjects that left the public relations major assigned to me very nervous. I got through all that comfortably, much to his surprise. He acted from the beginning as though this whole thing could never come off without his guidance and wisdom.

The next day my interviews were with the 5th Air Force and Far East Air Force (FEAF) commanders. A few words in each case about what to say and not say upon arrival in the States and some words of congratulation, and I was on my way back to Korea. I had a few days to pack, during which Captain Joe McConnell showed up. He had been my assistant flight commander at George. For several days at every opportunity Joe and I discussed every possible aspect of my tour and how he might do it better. And do it better he did! The new F-86s arrived about this time with more thrust and better turning capabilities and Joe McConnell made the best of it. When he went home he was the leading ace, with sixteen MiGs to his credit. Unfortunately, Joe was killed in an F-86H accident at Edwards in 1955 and we lost an absolutely outstanding fighter pilot.

My orders arrived and I spent what little time remained by packing and getting myself ready for return to the Land of the Big BX (Base Exchange). The night before I left there was a get-together for me at the officers' club and we all hoisted a few. Signs that read "Mukden 20 miles" (referring to my activities in Manchuria) and other key moments in my all-too-short tour were strewn about in the club. It was routine, I guess, for others. But to me it was the fulfillment of a dream that I had carried since I was barely old enough to ride a bicycle. When the last glass had been put on the bar and the club was dark, I made my way back to my quarters. I laid in my bunk staring out the window at more stars than I could ever remember seeing. The thought crossed my mind that for the last two days I had been receiving congratulations and thanks from the highest Air Force sources in the Pacific. Now it was my turn to put the credit where it really belonged. "Thank you, God," I muttered to myself, "for what measure of success you have given me these last few months and please give me the wisdom to take advantage of opportunities that may result from it." There were dozens of other things I wanted to say, but the next thing I knew someone was shaking me, saying my ride to the States left in one hour.

★ ★ ★

CHAPTER 11

Back to Work

I left Korea as a major but I arrived in the good old U.S.A. as a captain. My promotion in the combat zone was called a spot promotion, and as such was generally reserved for the theater of operations. This type of promotion had to be approved by the next regular promotion board, which unfortunately didn't meet until the following April. As a result, I reverted to captain from October 1952 until April 1953.

My orders came through assigning me to Nellis AFB, Nevada as an instructor in the Aircraft Gunnery Squadron. The assignment was great, but first I had to get to Phoenix to see my wife, my new daughter, Melanie, and my son, Kent.

Arriving in Phoenix, I was suddenly caught up in a flurry of requests for speeches, radio and personal appearances. A few days later, I found myself riding in an open convertible down the main street of Phoenix. People lined the street. The mayor had declared it "Captain Blesse Day" and presented me a key to the city. It was an exciting two or three weeks and I'll never forget it if I live to be two hundred.

At the appointed time, I reported to Nellis. It wasn't what I expected at first. Flight training was in full swing and I was expecting to get caught up in it as quickly as possible. Instead, the public-relations people in the Pentagon requested my presence and I left to make a couple of speeches. The program gained momentum and soon I was gone at least half of each month making speeches at colleges, service clubs, schools, organizations of all kinds—and some were pretty high class places. The day I addressed the Executive Club in Chicago I learned Dwight Eisenhower and Winston Churchill were previous speakers. By then, though, it was automatic—no shakes, no wondering about content. I had learned they wanted me to appear, and short of disgracing them and myself, whatever I talked about appeared to interest them. The key was to know what you were talking about.

I didn't mind speaking, except it took away a lot of my flying. The six squadrons combined were flying 15,000 hours a month at Nellis. It was busy as hell and everybody was needed. Even being gone half of each month, I was still flying thirty or thirty-five hours a month in the F-86.

After four or five months of public speaking, I went to the Pentagon and asked if they would let me go back to work as a fighter pilot. They agreed I had done my part and I went back to Nellis, relieved and ready to plunge into the fighter training program. My promotion to major was confirmed in April 1953 and soon I found myself operations officer of the Gunnery Squadron.

I held the job for about a year and then was sent down to the 3596th Flying Training Squadron as ops officer under Major Bill Whisner, a superior fighter pilot. After shooting down four aircraft over Germany one day late in the war, he returned to find his airfield under attack. Although he had already run out of fuel, he countered the attack of an aggressive German pilot and shot him down over the airfield and did it in time to successfully complete a dead-stick landing. Only the best of the best could pull that off. Anyway, Bill was a fine squadron commander and many months later it was with mixed emotions I learned of his impending transfer—even though I was to be the new commander.

In my previous job, we were working with seasoned veterans teaching them how to go back to their outfits and set up gunnery and tactics programs of their own. In the Flying Training Squadron, our mission was different. We were dealing now with new pilots, teaching them the skills they would need to survive in combat.

There was no shortage of experienced teachers. Nellis had been sent almost all of the jet aces and many other combat returnees from Korea. The problem was, they didn't all think alike. I'm guessing, but I think most of the aces felt pretty much like I did—that line-abreast formation was good for defense but not maneuverable enough for offensive action. If the aces had all been squadron commanders, our task of standardizing training among the six squadrons would have been much easier. As it turned out, for almost a year each squadron commander conducted training as he saw fit, and most of the time it differed in many respects from training in the other squadrons.

A series of events occurred to help change this, and one was formation of a squadron tactics team in my unit. We began flying against other flights in the squadron to see what kind of product we were turning out. There was interest from outside, and we began receiving requests to fly against other USAF squadrons. The word spread and soon Navy and Marine units were requesting we fly with them on the weekend. The tactics team had caught on. Today we have tactics teams called Aggressor Squadrons in three of our major commands—TAC, PacAF, and USAFE.

★ ★ ★

CHAPTER 12

The Gunnery Meet

While we were struggling for some standardization in our combat crew training program, the Air Force announced that in 1954 the worldwide fighter gunnery meet would be resumed. It was customary in the Air Force up until the Korean War to hold such competition, but after the 1950 meet the event was cancelled.

Colonel Bruce Hinton, later the Nellis group commander, described the gunnery contest and what it meant: "In this meet, the winning teams from each command competition, including U.S. Air Forces in Europe and the Pacific, came annually to pit the best fighter teams from everywhere in air-to-air and air-to-ground gunnery, skip- and dive-bombing, and rocketry. With no war to fight, this meet was the most important event in fighter aviation. Participation as a team member was a prime goal of every fighter pilot and ground-crew member. The ultimate goal of each pilot was to be a member of the winning team and in the process to take individual honors with the highest score in an individual phase such as air-to-air gunnery. The prestige in either case was peerless, establishing a permanent sense of deep accomplishment as well as an Air Force–wide reputation."

The 1954 meet was not to be held till June, but competition

began as early as March to decide who the five men would be to represent Nellis. Similar teams were being formed at other Air Training Command bases. It would be necessary to have a meet within Air Training Command to determine which base would represent the command. Teams also were forming in front-line tactical units in Asia, Europe, and the United States. I survived the Nellis eliminations, and Nellis won the right to compete in the Air Force meet by defeating teams from Luke, Williams, Laughlin, and others within Training Command. All of this involved several months of flying three or four missions a day in the hottest part of the year in Nevada—but we were ready.

A week before the meet, I returned home from flying to learn Dotty's father had suffered a stroke in Long Beach. We made immediate plans to hustle her off to help him. Returning home from the airport, I got a call from my sister saying my father had a heart attack in Richmond, Virginia, and wasn't expected to live. The station commander, General Jim Roberts, gave me an F-86 and said, "I know you have to go. See if you can get back in time for the meet." He said he would send a T-33 to follow in case I had any trouble. I got a babysitter for the two kids and off I went.

Six-hundred-mile legs coast to coast—three landings and refuelings—and at 0300 I was circling Byrd Field in Richmond asking for permission to land. I was advised they had no power unit to start an F-86 and that the runway was minimum satisfactory for jet traffic. I elected to land anyway. I had used an American Airlines power unit a year earlier to get started after putting on an air show there, so I knew a little about both of the major problems. I landed—it was really no problem—and must have had fifteen feet left over! They tucked my F-86 away for the night and I hustled into the hospital. Naturally, Dad was asleep, so I slept in a chair the rest of the night and wondered why the hell I didn't think this out more clearly when I was asking to land.

The next morning Dad looked good. He was out of his oxygen tent, making smart remarks at the nurses, and it looked like things would be okay. He was a great guy; I couldn't have had a better father. We talked most of the morning, both of us saying things we might not have said under other circumstances.

Late in the afternoon, after I slept four hours, the doctor said it should be safe enough for me to leave, so I headed for home. I still had no idea how Dotty's father was, and she didn't even know I wasn't home. I got back to Nellis early in the morning. Before I could get to bed my sister called and said Dad had another attack. I had to get some sleep before I started back. He died before I awoke. Dotty's father was partially paralyzed but he lived through his ordeal. It was quite a while before things returned to normal. In any event, the 1954 Air Force Gunnery Meet was over for me, but more importantly, the man who taught me it was a kid's job to honor his parents, his family, and his country was gone forever.

In January 1955, our Nellis tactics team was honored with a request from the Fighter Division in the Pentagon to tour the Far East. There were twelve F-86 squadrons in Asia and we were directed to visit them all, then send a report on what we found.

Up until this point I had been briefing the flights with a rather-hastily-prepared eight-page fact sheet. The Asian trip rendered the handout inadequate, so I began a more extensive coverage of the entire tactics problem, complete with cartoons to keep my bright-eyed, bushy-tailed fighter pilots from going to sleep before they finished it. I called in *No Guts, No Glory*. We had enough copies made to leave four with each squadron we visited, and off we went.

The manual was an instant success, and before long it could be found in practically every fighter squadron in the Air Force. It also helped to standardize tactics training at Nellis.

The tactics trip to Asia was a real eye-opener. Captain Pappy Liles, Lieutenants Dan Druen, Don Pasco, and I comprised the team. These pilots I picked from the already elite group at Nellis, and I felt they were the best in the Air Force. We all had from 1,600 to 3,000 hours in the F-86 (unheard-of amounts then) and all had seen plenty of combat in Korea. Pappy Liles had some World War II combat as well. Dan Druen had only 1,600 hours in the F-86, so I put him in charge of baggage. However, he was put in charge of a lot more before he left the Air Force; he retired as a three-star general.

We visited twelve squadrons in Japan, Korea, and the Philippines, including one F-86 squadron on Taiwan at the request of the Chief of Staff of the Taiwanese Air Force, General "Tiger" Wong. In general, except for one squadron at Itazuke, Japan, the Chinese squadron on Taiwan, and one squadron in Korea, the units were relatively unprepared for air-to-air combat.

After a thorough report on our findings, some significant changes occurred. Not the least of these was the firing of two wing commanders and the changing of dozens of jobs throughout the command. I checked behind every door for weeks.

The tactics team did a lot to advance the ideas we advocated, and soon the new group commander at Nellis, Colonel Hinton, saw to it that training was standardized in accordance with the principles laid out in *No Guts, No Glory*. He was very mission-oriented; he'd been the first F-86 pilot to bag a MiG. But Nellis was only one of three bases training fighter pilots for combat. Luke and Williams Air Force Bases in Arizona had their own ideas, too. The solution to that problem came later.

The four of us on the tactics team had barely hung up our G-suits when preparations for the 1955 gunnery meet began. Although it was May, there was ample time because this year the meet would be in October. The initial thirty-five picked were the best each squadron had. In two or three weeks of recording every round fired, every bomb dropped, every rocket launched, the number had dwindled to about twenty. More competition, more recording of scores, another three weeks and the number was ten, then seven.

More competition, this time for a longer period of time, and finally it got down to five: Tommy Tapper, Pappy Liles, Homer Charleton, Cal Davey, and myself. Our team captain was a full colonel, a hard-driving, highly competitive fighter pilot named "Red" Grumbles. From May 1955 till the meet in October, we flew three or four missions a day—strafing and skip-bombing on the early mission when the air was smooth; rocket firing and dive-bombing in the later morning and then two air-to-air gunnery missions in the afternoon. After a couple of months of this, Red laid out the organization of the team. The rules required the team captains to compete only against each other and to fly all events. Pappy Liles and Tommy Tapper were designated our ground specialists, like I had been the year before. Homer Charleton and Cal Davey were to specialize in air-to-air. I was chosen to compete in all events. With the extensive practice we had, any one of us could have flown in all events. From that time on, the practice schedule changed to reflect our assignments.

As noted, in August we received a new Fighter Training Group Commander, Colonel Bruce Hinton. Young, capable, and a superior fighter pilot, he was fresh out of the Pentagon. His evaluation of the USAF, TAC, and finally Nellis itself, is worth noting:

"By the mid-1950s, the U.S. Air Force had grown in a dramatic surge from the emaciated condition following World War II. In 1955 the Air Force was over three times the size it was in 1947 and at the highest level it would ever be in the years after that right up to today.

"Tactical Air Command was reconstituted and growing rapidly with the assignment of fighter and fighter-bomber wings and squadrons in the wake of the Korean War. The Air Force overseas theaters were also growing, particularly in Europe and the Pacific, settling into the long haul of the Cold War.

"New aircraft were also coming in, with the improved F-86 models, F-84 series, and the F-100. F-105s were imminent, and the F-104 was on its way. Tactical air was taking on its new shape against the threat crystallized by Korea, a threat now identified with development of advanced high-performance fighters and bombers, aggressive intentions, and the atomic bomb.

"Nellis Air Force Base by 1955 had become the heart and soul of fighters for tactical air. Under command of the Crew Training Air Force (CrewTAF), Nellis received graduate pilots out of the flying schools as commissioned officers destined for day fighters and put them through air and ground training to emerge as qualified fighter pilots. The demand for fighter pilots was at a peak, requiring tightly compacted training and extremely heavy flying schedules. In fact, at the main gate a prominent sign read, 'Welcome to Nellis Air Force Base, Home of the Fighter Pilot,' and underneath that, 'The Busiest Airfield in the World.'

"On the ramp when I arrived at Nellis were over 400 fighters, mostly F-86E and F-86F models with some F-100s and T-33s. Fighter training was organized within the 3595th Combat Crew Training Group, which had six training squadrons supported by a ground training organization and an instrument-flying school. The CCT squadrons were commanded by highly experienced fighter pilots in the grade of major and organized as closely as possible to a fighter squadron in the field with an operations officer and flights of instructors. The difference lay in assignment of a group of students to each instructor, bringing the total number of pilots in each squadron to several times that of a squadron in the field within a tactical wing.

"It was one of these combat crew training squadrons, the 3596th, which I found Major Frederick C. Blesse commanding when I arrived at Nellis and assumed command of the 3595th Combat Crew Training Group in August 1955.

"I would like to mention that I felt the assignment to command the group at Nellis was the most choice of any in the U.S. Air Force, particularly for a relatively junior colonel fighter pilot. Nellis was known throughout the world as representing the highest level of professional fighter skill and knowledge. Here would be the elite of fighter pilots and an opportunity to be a part of this renowned organization. It was also here at Nellis that these elite fighter pilots would compete in the worldwide gunnery meet.'' Indeed, it was already happening.

By late September we were all doing very well. It was difficult to know how well, because we didn't know how the other teams were doing. In any event, we were about as sharp as we were going to get. Since May, I had flown over 250 hours in the same F-86.

Colonel Hinton knew we were locked in a competitive struggle and remembered it this way: ''The Nellis team was working long hours preparing for the meet. The morning sun peeked over Sunrise Mountain just east of the base, painting long shadows of the blue motor scooters heading for team operations. I think the whole team had those scooters painted with the 3596th Squadron colors. Missions went out all morning followed by afternoon on the harmonization range, firing in new .50 caliber machine guns or mounts and harmonizing the gunsights. There was constant maintenance on the F-86s to smooth out controls, recheck electrical systems, peak up gunsights and radars; an endless list of things to get a small edge in performance. Run the film from the gunsight aiming point camera for angle off, range, tracking smoothness; check dive angles; pipper creeping on the target, wind corrections, range at release, and on and on. Then recheck the film one more time. And planning for peaking out pilots, airplanes, parts needed, cross-training ground crew members (limited by meet rules to a minimum) to assist in case of urgent repairs or maintenance during the meet. The team operations area was compared to an anthill of activity overlaying an ordered necessity.''

I wanted to know what it was going to take to win, so I dug into the files and began looking over past years' performances. I found some very interesting data. The overall winner of the meet every year had a zero in at least one event. This was caused by fouling out—too low on a skip-bomb pass, firing past the foul line on a strafing run, pulling out too low from a rocket or dive-bomb run, or firing at too low an angle on the air-to-air towed target. What causes this? Too eager! Too determined to do something better today than ever before. I couldn't help but note how easy it would have been to have the same total without any zero events. I took each event and assigned a score to it—a score on which I would bet fifty dollars of my own money. That obviously wasn't going to be the best I had ever done or anything even close to it. It was a score I could make easily every day of the week—one that created no pressure inside, no feeling that everything had to be perfect.

When I completed my tabulation, I totaled the score and got the surprise of my life—it surpassed all previous records and would have established a new meet record. My confidence soared! I wrote a letter a week before the Air Force Worldwide Gunnery Meet, addressed it to my wife, and put it in a strong-box, not to be opened until after the meet was over. Essentially, I said I would not only win individual honors in the meet but I would establish an all-time high score in the process. Did I think I was that much better than all other pilots? Of course not; any of the pilots on our team could have done the same thing. I just knew that a pilot flying with no pressure could beat one trying to do his all-time best on every pass during a week-long competition.

The meet was conducted with its usual efficiency. Nellis was flooded with dignitaries from all over the world watching the fighter units as they competed for the U.S. Air Force Championship.

Our team did what we all hoped for. We won the championship just as we had the year before, and our leader, Colonel Red Grumbles, won the team captain's trophy. Me? It worked out pretty much as I thought. I did win the trophy offered for individual performance. I did set a new all-time record as I predicted. Another thing happened, though, which has since become a matter of great pride. I won every single trophy offered for individual performance—a feat that to this day has never been equalled. I couldn't have done that with the average scores I estimated. As a result of having no pressure to reach the standards I had set for myself, I did much better—in some cases, as well as I had ever done. To this day, I use that philosophy in golf tournaments and other forms of competition. It really works.

I didn't know it at the time, but the new group commander was watching me. He said later, "Soon after I arrived at Nellis, the name of 'Boots' Blesse was mentioned more often as the leading team pilot to watch. During the week-long, worldwide meet, this proved to be true. Boots Blesse not only became the key man contributing to the Nellis team winning overall, but he individually won first place in all events. It was a spectacular accomplishment which I believe has not been equalled in any other meet.

"Not long after getting settled in at Nellis, I was holding a weekly conference of squadron commanders and key supervisors of flying and training. The intensity of operations demanded constant attention and improvement in scheduling, flight safety, curriculum changes, and, in particular, operational procedures. I was running through a list of items to be accomplished and explaining in some detail how to go about getting the changes across to the pilots in the squadrons when Boots interrupted, saying, 'Colonel, why not just tell us what you want done, then let us figure out how we will do it.'

"Blesse, capable, confident in his capabilities, was throwing a challenge not just at me but at every other squadron commander present. It was refreshing, and made my job a lot easier. Now all that remained was for him to prove he could fulfill his statement.

"In the months that followed, I found that attitude was Boots's trademark. He was a dedicated, disciplined officer who never disobeyed orders, but as long as room existed for suggestion, discussion, or new ideas, he spoke up. He had an alert, creative mind which continued to show in his squadron activities and various features of his squadron operations. And he seemed to be one of those people who did almost everything well.

"One day in conversation about playing golf with another officer, I was told that Boots was almost a scratch golfer. The other officer went on to say that Boots had never played until recently but he went out and became practically an overnight expert, due, as he told me, to Boots's natural ability to do anything well. Although I found he actually was very good at the game, I never uncovered whether that remark about his being new at the game was just another one of those stories arising around Boots or was actually true. That does, however, show the kind of superman aura which was accorded him by those at Nellis.

"Several times Boots initiated discussions about tactics. His experience in the Korean War resulted in publication of *No Guts, No Glory* as his kind of individual fighter tactical doctrine. But to him, that was a step along the way toward refining the art of air-to-air fighting through maneuvering by thinking ahead of the enemy and planning the moves to be made.

"I recall meeting him one afternoon as I left my office when we spent a long hour in a heated discussion on the relative values of defensive versus offensive tactics and maneuvering. He knew his side of the matter, and since it was a free discussion, he expressed his views with a positive, articulate conviction. I was arguing against some of those views with what I thought were convincing points. After a long while, we closed it out but I don't think I changed his mind one bit. It was the same tenacity and concentration which made him the leader he proved to be."

The time at Nellis whizzed by. The flying was the greatest in the world. As I mentioned, the training program gradually became centralized under Colonel Hinton, and life was about as good as it could be if you liked flying fighters.

Unfortunately, about this time centralized maintenance raised its ugly head. We had been using "organizational maintenance." Under that system, a crew chief was assigned to a specific aircraft, and all the things he needed to do his work, except extensive rebuilds, were assigned to the squadron. When you deployed to another base, you took it all with you. The centralized maintenance system relegated the crew chief to a refueling specialist. All repair work was done by crews assigned to centralized sections. These sections served all three squadrons in the wing.

Though it was pretty good for bombers that usually returned to the base with their specialists, centralized maintenance was slightly better than a disaster for fighter units. We normally deployed one squadron at a time, and some specialists had to go with each squadron. By the time the last squadron in the wing deployed, there was not enough support left to give adequate maintenance.

SAC was in control, however, and not to be denied. The new program was forced upon us as a management tool, and the base flying-hour output promptly dropped from about 14,000 hours per month to 8,000 and never recovered. Happily, centralized maintenance in tactical wings has since been replaced with a system very similar to what we had previously—mechs with red hats working on airplanes with red squadron stripes, or yellow or blue. Morale also improved.

In 1954 and 1955 I wrote letters to Air Training Command Headquarters explaining the evils that centralized maintenance would create in a fighter unit. Another letter suggested the Aircraft Gunnery Squadron have at least one or two teams that taught fighter tactics since it was a far more important thing to know than the mere technique of positioning the gunsight pipper on the target. Other letters followed from time to time—not dissenting letters necessarily, just information letters that outlined how I felt about special subjects, just in case anyone wanted to know.

The lightweight fighter was such a topic. I felt we should specialize and build an aircraft that was only for air-to-air fighting, and also build a fighter-bomber that didn't have to do anything but attack targets. When one aircraft has to do both jobs, there are too many compromises.

The dart target was another gripe. To me it was worthless to spend money on darts and waste missions firing at them when those missions don't simulate the real world. The best training you can get is using a gun camera while you are maneuvering against another aircraft. Firing 20mm guns is expensive—the only reason you have to fire a gun these days is to ensure the gun will fire and that your rounds will go where the sight says they are supposed to. Maintenance test pilots can do that. Pilots can never get enough air-to-air training, and what they do get needs to be maneuvering against other aircraft using a gunsight for verification of technique in the debriefing. I never got much of a reaction from any of the letters except the one on centralized maintenance. I got a phone call advising me to keep my opinions on that subject to myself.

During the summer of 1955 I had been appointed technical adviser on a movie called *Sabre Jet*. One day I got a midmorning phone call from Los Angeles asking me to come down ASAP to review some film. I jumped in an F-86 right after lunch and headed for LAX. The Air Force kept a small maintenance contingent at Los Angeles International, and they took good care of me as soon as I landed. The only piece of navigational equipment on the F-86 was what we call a radio compass. You could tune in any radio station and the needle would point to the station. My radio compass was inoperative on the flight down, so I told the crew chief I wanted to return to Nellis before dark. He assured me the bird would be ready to go when I got back.

By late afternoon I had finished at the film studio and raced for the airport. Shadows were lengthening. A different crew had the power unit plugged in and was all set when I drove up.

A quick walk around the aircraft revealed that it still had wings and a tail, so I hurried up the ladder, checked the pins on the ejection seat, and slid into the cockpit. Seat belt and shoulder harness fastened, I ran quickly over the rest of the checks because the sun was disappearing behind the Pacific Ocean. That meant it would be dark in about thirty minutes. The engine struggled to life and I began taxiing to the active runway, which was number twenty-seven. The traffic was at an afternoon low for Los Angeles International Airport, so as I approached the runway the tower cleared me for a running takeoff. I remember thinking how quick the F-86 got airborne at sea level. There was only an 1,800-foot difference in altitude between Nellis and Los Angeles, but I wasn't to be confused by facts at the moment. I just wanted to get back before dark.

A 180° turn and I was climbing up through the low layer of clouds that hung over the airport. At about 10,000 feet, I broke out of the clouds and casually observed a couple of airliners climbing out. The air was smooth as silk. It was so peaceful. As a matter of routine my eyes scanned the gauges in the cockpit and then tried to resume their usual search in the sky for other aircraft. "Jesus Christ!" The world's fastest double take jerked my eyes back to the fuel gauge. "There's no goddamn fuel in this bird!" As I wracked the Sabre into a 180° turn, I switched channels on the radio to get Radar Approach Control. I could see the fuel-gauge needle resting on about 200 pounds. If I didn't touch the throttle I might make the field; one try, that's all.

I began descending. No radio compass, so all I could do was take the reciprocal of my climbout heading. Let's see. I made a sweeping left turn after takeoff before starting my climb, so I should break out of the overcast south of the field. "Radar Approach, Air Force 207. I've got engine trouble. I'm returning to LA International. Request Vector." No answer. "Approach Control, if you copy, this is Air Force 207. I'm at 7,000, heading 260°, letting down." No answer. I switched to tower frequency. "Los Angeles Tower, Air Force 207, do you read?" Before the tower could answer, I broke out underneath the clouds. By now it was dark. Everything was a sea of lights. I scanned the area for the airport, concentrating to my right. Nothing but lights.

"Air Force 207, LA Tower. You got a problem?"

"Roger, Tower. Does a rat have a tail? Are your runway lights on?"

"Tower here, that's affirmative."

A glance at my airspeed—decreased to 350. Fuel gauge zero, but the engine was still running. "Blink 'em," I shot back, "I don't have you." I scanned in near panic. Christ, I thought, I'm too low to make the water. This thing's going to end up in someone's backyard if something doesn't happen. Then I saw those beautiful blinking lights—north of me, like I figured. A quick turn and a moment later I was in the pattern, throttle right where I put it at 11,000 feet—all the way back. It was a good long runway so I made it without throttle and coasted to a taxiway near the end of the runway. "Jesus, that was close. Where's that fuckin' crew chief!"

Before I found him, I had time to think about whose fault it really was. I was the one who took the aircraft and it was my responsibility to know its condition. In a few minutes the crew chief arrived on the tow vehicle, half expecting me to want to kill him, but I felt so stupid all I could muster were a few words about how lucky I was I didn't bust my ass. I packed it in. I'd had enough excitement for one day. Now, I just wanted a good night's sleep. The next day I was back at Nellis teaching students how to properly check their aircraft before flight.

In the summer of 1955, while we were preparing for the gunnery meet, I successfully dodged a bullet from Major General "Moose" Stillman for me to join the initial cadre of the new Air Force Academy. I had taken over as squadron commander of the 3596th "Cadillac" Squadron at Nellis, and we were going to convert to F-100s. I conveyed this to General Stillman in a letter, along with some other reasons for staying where I was. I got a very terse reply which I have saved to this day. It said, "I read your letter with tearstained eyes. Request is withdrawn. Don't stay in the cockpit so long you forget other things are going on in the Air Force." He was an outstanding officer and, to be completely honest about it, I might have been smart to accept his offer.

CHAPTER 13

Randolph

One bullet I didn't dodge came eight months later in the form
of a reassignment to Crew Training Air Force Headquarters at
Randolph AFB, Texas. I reported to Randolph as assistant
chief of the Fighter Division in early 1956. Lieutenant Colonel
Ed Cunningham was the chief. Ed was killed in a T-33 accident
a short time later and I replaced him. I brought in Captain Joe
Smith from Nellis and Captain Aaron Bowman from Luke to
increase our experience level, then went to work trying to
standardize the fighter training in CTAF.

After eight months of briefings and explanations at top level,
we finally got a modified version of *No Guts, No Glory* out as
a CTAF manual. This finally standardized the fighter training
at all three bases. It was during this period we coined the
phrase "Air Combat Maneuvering."

The word "tactics," like "dogfighting," had a hint of reck-
lessness in it, and any mention of training with those terms was
doomed to failure. "Air Combat Maneuvering" seemed to
command respect, so we went with that and it stuck.

Directing a change in tactics training was one thing, but
getting people to do it properly was an entirely different matter.
I spent about half of my time traveling to Luke, Williams, and
Nellis, flying with the product they were turning out. The first
month or two we had only T-33s for travel but General H. R.

Spicer, the new Commander of Crew Training, brought six F-86s with him. He established a very high requirement of Sabre time for base pilots to be allowed to fly '86s, so I was able to get one anytime I needed it. It was good to arrive in a fighter with the job I had. It made things so much easier.

One day on the way into Williams AFB near Phoenix, I was enjoying the beautiful flying weather at 35,000 feet—smooth air and light jet wind. Suddenly, I noticed a lack of power. The tail pipe temperature (TPT) began increasing and I had to further decrease power to stay within safe operating limits. Soon I had a vibration and pulled the throttle to idle. TPT was still max allowable so I shut down the engine completely.

I was only about sixty miles out and had plenty of altitude, so I decided I would glide toward the base and set up a possible dead-stick landing. Student flying was in full swing, so there was no way to know what condition the runway would be in on arrival. Fortunately, things worked out. I got over the base and got one more dead-stick landing using our procedures from Korea. The fire trucks followed me on landing, and when I stopped, they rolled up and motioned me to get the hell out of the aircraft—it was burning in the rear end. They didn't have to tell me twice!

However, I had to tell General Spicer—twice—about engine oil seals and how they sometimes fail. Since it wasn't my fault, I stayed on his golden list of authorized pilots for the F-86.

Two years of Randolph was great. Super quarters, a pool, nice club and golf course—that base had it all.

At Randolph, our third child and second daughter, Angelie, arrived. Christian, our fourth, made it two and two when he arrived in June of 1958. Unfortunately, the bubble burst and I was transferred to Germany several months before Christian was born, so I wasn't around for his debut.

★ ★ ★

CHAPTER 14

Boom Boom

I went to Europe in March 1958 after a gruelling month at survival school near Reno, Nevada. On arrival in Europe I was assigned to the 36th Tactical Fighter Wing at Bitburg, Germany. The wing was equipped with F-100C Super Sabres and, since I had little time in the F-100, I was sent to the 32d Fighter Squadron in North Africa to fly with them awhile. The objective was to become familiar with wing operations.

The 32d Fighter Squadron usually was stationed at Soesterberg Air Base in Holland, but because of the bad weather this time of year in Europe, they were on their customary deployment to Morocco to increase flying time and improve training in general. On my first day of flying there was trouble. After a very thorough introduction, the briefing officer announced we would log two hours on this flight. With no external tanks on the F-100C, it was not feasible for the mission we were about to fly, and I brought that to his attention. His answer was, "We log two hours with a clean aircraft and three if we have external tanks installed."

I didn't know much but I knew that wasn't right. The briefing officer suggested I talk to the ops officer or commander for an official explanation as to why that was being done. The explanation made sense but it didn't make it right. The European command received a certain allocation of flying hours each year—if all those hours weren't flown, the next year's allocation would be smaller. No one wanted that, so in the 32d Squadron every effort was being made to log the time whether it was actually being flown or not. I was told if I was not comfortable with that to log my flying as I saw fit, and that is exactly what I did. I also made a note to myself to check wing policy when I got back to Bitburg and see what was written on the subject. I was in an ideal position because the wing commander had informed his staff he was forming a Tactical Evaluation Section, and that I would be part of it. It would be our job, then, to ensure all squadrons were flying in accordance with existing regulations.

Transition complete, I returned to Bitburg. I made no big issue of the time-logging incident, but I did make it a part of our tactical procedure to check the accuracy of flight hours logged in each unit we visited. I didn't care what they had been doing, I just wanted it done right from now on.

Preparation continued for our first tactical evaluation visit, and when we were only a few weeks away from leaving, I got a call to go see the wing commander. He asked me why I had mentioned the business about checking flying time. I told him I did it because I wasn't sure it was being done properly in all squadrons, and if it wasn't, it would be a reflection on him. He asked, "Do you have any reason to think it was not being done properly?"

"Yes, sir," I replied, and told him of my experience with the 32d Squadron in Morocco. It was duly noted and some time later he sent an investigator to Soesterberg (Camp New Amsterdam) to look into the matter.

Meanwhile, I got an accelerated promotion to lieutenant colonel, "below the zone." That was April 1958.

The events of the next few weeks were to give me the best job an L-C could have in the European theater, but they also were to shatter my relationship with the wing commander, and, along with some other things, ensured that I stayed a light colonel for a good long time.

The 36th TFW commander was a full colonel who was five feet six inches of pure dynamite, known as "Boom Boom." He was a bright, capable, dedicated, aggressive officer and a highly qualified fighter pilot. He was a good athlete who enjoyed a tough game of squash several times a week as long as it didn't interfere with his Saturday golf game. He made things happen. He ran the wing in every sense of the word and had his finger in the selection of all key supervisory personnel, even in the off-base squadrons. It seemed to me no one did anything without his approval. I liked him, and got to know him pretty well because he quickly learned I was the only one who could beat him in squash and golf. With all his good attributes he was still explosive and unpredictable, hence the nickname "Boom Boom."

One morning he called me in and asked me to develop a plan and briefing for conducting a twenty-four-hour airborne alert with fighters carrying nuclear weapons. I worked on it constantly for three or four days, and when I was satisfied with it I got on his calendar and gave him a briefing. He sat back in his chair with his feet on his desk and the usual cigar in his mouth, puffing approval as I made my way from one point to the next. When I finished, I was delighted to see him smiling with approval.

Now, up to this point the colonel never asked me what I thought about the idea—he merely asked me to develop the briefing. Suddenly, in a wave of satisfaction he said, "Fine, fine, Blesse, what do you think about me giving this to General LeMay when he visits next month?" All I could think of was the number of single-engine fighters I had flown that developed oil leaks, gas leaks, control problems, engine failures, instrument failure at night, etc., and my thought was one of relief that none of these had a nuclear weapon hanging underneath. I finally turned toward the wing commander, who was obviously awaiting an answer, and said, "Sir, you'd have to be out of your mind to give the Chief of Staff a briefing like this."

I had barely gotten the words out of my mouth when Boom

Boom blew that lighted cigar about eight feet over the desk and onto the wall-to-wall carpeting. While I was stamping out sparks, he was shouting at me. "What do you mean out of my mind—if I want your opinion, I'll ask for it!"

I calmly said, although I didn't feel too calm, "Sir, I thought you did ask me for it."

Only the words, "Out! Out!" could be heard, and they could be heard everywhere. The colonel was motioning me out of his office—face red, arms waving wildly, but I felt he was saying out of Germany, out of the Air Force. I never had anyone in the Air Force yell at me before.

I hurried back to my office and there sat Jack Rattie, a super guy I was working for, laughing his ass off. "You and the boss have a little difference of opinion?" he asked.

"Yeah," I said, "I made the mistake of thinking he really wanted to know what I thought of the nuclear airborne alert plan." Jack headed for the door. As he left the room he turned and said, "Don't let it get to you. Forget it, it's just part of old Boom Boom's charm." That was easy for him to say, since it was me the commander was shouting at!

The next morning I felt like I would just as soon not go to work. When I arrived I knew it was a mistake, for on my desk was a note from the commander's office. I unfolded it expecting the worst, but Boom Boom wanted to meet me for squash in the gym at 1600. No package of Rolaids ever gave relief like that.

With a couple of squash games a week and golf on the weekend, we eventually developed a good relationship. The colonel called me "Boots" and I called him "sir." Seriously, you couldn't help but like him; he had a good sense of humor, he was a Shakespearean actor when he needed to be, and he was constantly working to make his wing the best in the theater.

The summer raced by. It comes and goes quickly in Europe, and if you blink you'll miss it. Personnel changes were routine in the summer because families had to get back to the Land of the Big BX and get the kids ready for school. The commander at Soesterberg in Holland was an exception. He was to rotate in the early fall, and the wing commander asked if I wanted that job. He didn't have to ask twice. So during late summer and early fall, although I was working in the wing HQ at Bitburg, Germany, I knew I was to be the new CO of Camp New Amsterdam, Soesterberg Air Base.

Suddenly a series of events propelled me into the commander's job almost before I was ready. In my position I only knew what spilled over from the top, but apparently the colonel didn't like what he heard from the investigator who went to Camp New Amsterdam, and he fired the 32d Squadron's commander. The issue was overlogging of flying time. The squadron commander was ordered to meet what is called a 36-2 Board, which essentially says, "This had been alleged; prove to me it is not true." Testimony was taken, witnesses interviewed, all the data was sifted through, and finally the board decided against the squadron commander and he was required to leave the service. This was a real shocker because he was an extremely capable officer, well liked by the Dutch as well as his American counterparts and, from all indications, he was doing a superior job.

★ ★ ★

CHAPTER 15

Soesterberg

When I first took over at Camp New Amsterdam, I was surprised at the complexity of the job. I couldn't help wondering if I had gotten in over my head. I had been a squadron commander before, but here, over and above the squadron responsibilities, I had a dentist, a doctor, motor pool, hospital, NCO and officer clubs, various funds, military police, and a host of other activities that are all a part of a large base complex. Reporting procedures were a nightmare. Our squadron was operationally under control of the Dutch, logistically and administratively under the 36th Tactical Fighter Wing at Bitburg, and, in several other areas such as air police and medical care, we answered directly to Headquarters, United States Air Forces in Europe (USAFE), quartered in Wiesbaden, Germany. After about a year or so we were taken completely away from the 36th TFW and transferred to the 86th TFW at Ramstein, Germany. That improved things somewhat but it was still a sporty course.

As soon as I arrived at Camp New Amsterdam (which was one side of the Dutch base of Soesterberg) I began an inspection of all the different activities—a project that took me the better part of two weeks. When I had finished, there was no doubt in my mind I had a problem on my hands that was a lot more serious than the recording of flying time.

No one had anything but the best of intentions in trying to protect the flying-hour allocation, but the unknown implications that followed were catastrophic. From a daily operating standpoint, it falsified our squadron supply situation. Of a much more serious nature, it weakened the standards of integrity, and people—pushed by the pressure of barely achievable goals—found easier ways of achieving those goals. Parachute inspections, engine work, parts delivery, flying time, and a host of other things were simply not being done in accordance with regulations. The record was there but the performance was not.

It seems like a simple enough problem: find out who is involved and fire them. Well, it wasn't quite that easy. First, and probably most important, was that the wing commander, who was an aggressive, strong leader, was directly involved in the selection of these people. I anticipated great resistance in actually trying to remove any of them. I am not insinuating the "Wing King" was stacking the deck with people he could control, I just mean people were doing things he didn't have any way of knowing about. After all, we were about two hundred miles from Bitburg. I felt strongly that the people involved—about eight of them—really needed to be removed if we were going to start fresh and convince everyone things were going to be done right. My alternative was to try to run the base with people in supervisory positions who knew they couldn't be fired. I found that unacceptable. While I was looking for an answer, another problem involving parts to keep our fighters flying put me on a collision course with the commander and his staff at Bitburg.

In a tactical fighter squadron, parts availability to a great extent is determined by past performance. We look at our recent record and anticipate what parts and how many will be required to fly a given number of hours. You can see readily that if a unit was flying 500 hours a month but logging 650, there is no way they can really fly 650 hours a month without changing their supply procedures. They simply would run out of parts. When that happens, planes became what we called AOCP—aircraft out of commission for parts. Now the wing commander had an ingenious program to inspire outside supply agencies all over the theater to service him better. He had gone a long time—about eighteen or twenty days—without an AOCP in the wing. He publicized that, and as the record number of days increased, no supply agency wanted to bear the responsibility of breaking the "no AOCP" record. The record grew, the service got better and better, and apparently everyone was working overtime to preserve it.

The record was in the hundreds of days when I took over at Soesterberg. I could see there was no possible way for us to operate without ending up the bastard at the family reunion. We were supposed to fly 650 hours a month, and as we tried to do that we flat ran out of parts. What was next? That's right—we reported an AOCP. The fight started as soon as the report reached Bitburg. I got a call from the director of Materiel, who showed me beyond all logic why it wasn't necessary to report this AOCP. A conversation like this between a junior lieutenant colonel and a senior full colonel involved very little beyond a lot of "Yes, sir" until he finally said, "This is the way to report."

At that I agreed to report any way he desired. I only asked one thing of him. I politely pointed out that USAF regulation 65–110 stated if the part wasn't on the base where the aircraft was located, the aircraft was to be reported AOCP. At present that was the only thing I had in writing that told me how to report parts shortages. I stressed that I was perfectly willing to report his way if he would just send me something in writing. He promised he would, but I never received anything. Within a week we had four or five aircraft AOCP and I was on the wing's "most wanted" list. The whole incident just proved to me how important it was that I clean house and get this base operating on a different standard.

Predictions were already flying that I wouldn't be around too long, and that gave me an idea that signed my death warrant with the commander and his staff; however, it also gave me the solution I was searching for. There was a regulation that said an officer couldn't receive a performance rating unless he had been under the rater's supervision at least 120 days. Three weeks had already zipped by, but that left me over three months to shape up the squadron. The way I saw it, one of two things would happen—either I would get fired or I wouldn't. Knowing the wing commander and taking into consideration the "former no-AOCP record," I wasn't betting any big money on my chances of remaining as squadron CO.

I did do one smart thing just before I launched my program to reshape Camp New Amsterdam; I completed a list of all the integrity violations I had uncovered during my inspection of the base. I put these violations in a carefully worded teletype report (TWX) and sent it to the wing commander at Bitburg. I was very careful to mark the TWX "Personal, Commander's Eyes Only" so he would know that only he and I knew the nature of the violations. This gave him an option. He could leave me alone and be reasonably sure the violations that occurred during his watch would not be made public and would be corrected. His other option was to fire me, in which case the condition of the base would surely become a matter of official record. It would be impossible to avoid one of us discussing such a subject in any action on his part to remove me. Armed with that shaky rationale, I called in my new operations officer, Major Bill Yancey, explained what I was going to do, and advised him he might be the new commander before long.

The next day I fired six key people (two operations personnel had already been replaced) and told them to report to Bitburg for new assignments the following Monday morning.

On Monday I got a call from the wing commander and, to say the least, he was unhappy as hell. He didn't need the telephone; I could have heard him from Bitburg without it. It was a long, unpleasant conversation and I kept waiting for the words, "Pack your bags," but they never came. It was not a pleasant feeling to know your boss would like to see you dead, but taking everything into consideration it could have been worse since I didn't get fired.

I let a week go by, and there was no word from Bitburg, so I decided to get on with the changes I wanted, and pretended I was going to be there a long time.

I called in all the key personnel and we discussed logging of flying time, reporting of aircraft in commission, parachute inspections and inspections of all kinds, supply reporting procedures, and the standards expected during the conduct of our everyday business. For a junior lieutenant colonel who thought he might be in over his head, I found myself in complete and total control. For a short time no one did anything without asking. I asked a lot of questions myself, got a lot of advice, and before long felt comfortable in my new role.

However, my relationship with the wing staff at Bitburg continued to worsen—claims of who said what to whom—until finally I put a recorder on my office phone and let it be known I would take calls from off-base on that phone only. I just kept getting in deeper and deeper. I didn't want to cause trouble. I didn't hate anybody. I just wanted to make the old 32d Fighter Squadron the best in the Air Force.

The first year flew by. I had pulled in a maintenance captain who was an ex-GI and made him my squadron executive officer. When I wasn't in the office, my "right arm," old John Taylor, was running things. I could never have made it without John to relieve me of the many details required in the administration of the base. During my command we expanded from about 280 people to almost 900. Most of that occurred when we converted from a day fighter mission to one involving air defense. We lost our F-100Cs and picked up F-102s in mid-1960.

Just as John Taylor was my right arm in the headquarters building, Bill Yancey was the pillar of reliability and responsibility in operations. I fought hard to get Bill to the 32d—he was a superior pilot and an outstanding officer in every sense of the word. From the beginning I asked for Bill but another officer was offered to me. Each of the three times this occurred, I told the wing commander I could make it satisfactorily with the officer he was suggesting but the man I really wanted was Bill Yancey. Finally, I got a call and was involved in a conversation during which I never said a word. I picked up the phone and the wing CO said, "All right, dammit, I'm sending you Yancey and I hope you're finally satisfied!" Before I could thank him, he hung up. Hanging in there for Bill was one of my smarter moves at Soesterberg.

We started lots of new things the first year. First it was the parades. I learned many of the airmen hadn't even drawn a blue uniform from supply. It seemed wrong to me to have airmen come and go and never get out of their fatigues, so once a month we conducted a parade in blues. John Taylor nearly went crazy but he and the supply officer finally got it squared away, and, over a period of time, the quality of the parades was such the dependents began coming to see them, then later some of our Dutch friends.

In operations we instituted what we called a tactical inspection. Once a month all the flyable aircraft were lined up on the taxiway, and beside each one was the pilot assigned to the aircraft, the crew chief, and the armorer. The operations officer, the maintenance officer, and the line chief and I would troop the line and supposedly pick out the best-looking aircraft. Actually, the line chief would give me the winner the night before to be sure we didn't pick a new-looking aircraft with a mediocre crew chief. That does bad things for morale. Most of the time the inspection would end with an order from me to fly 'em and we would generate a nice fly-by over the base.

I designated Friday afternoon for weekly base inspection. At about 1500 hours I would take a staff car with my first sergeant and John Taylor and literally go into each office on the base. Desktops had to be clear and drawers staggered open. It was just another way of saying we had standards at Soesterberg that must be met. I needed a symbol of authority, so I got an Air Force swagger stick—in fact, I had over a dozen of them.

When I was irritated over a repeated discrepancy I would crash the stick down in such a way to snap the head off of it. I'm sure many people thought I was a white-jacket case but it served the purpose nicely.

Then there was the squadron insignia. I started something that proved to be popular with the Dutch as well as our own people. We had a standard circular emblem with a wolfhound in the center. The Dutch, on the other hand, had a beautiful circular wreath with a crown on top, and each of their squadrons had their insignia in the center of it. Why not our wolfhound in the center, too? After all, we were operationally under control of Holland. The Dutch approved the idea and, without falling into the trap of trying to get USAF approval, we launched the program and became one of the "Queen's finest." As I recall that was in 1959.

As all these things were adjusting attitudes, we began solving our flying problems. In a TWX to the wing commander, I estimated we would not make our flying commitment for about three months while we reestablished our supply base. That worked about as we forecast, and once we got on our feet, we had little trouble flying our 650 to 700 hours a month.

Each year while we had F-100s, we sent a detachment to Wheelus Air Base, Libya, for gunnery. The weather was so bad in Europe that we needed the extra training and flying time. During one of our deployments we had two pilots that ran into trouble coming from Holland to Libya and ended up ejecting over the water. One was picked up quickly, the other we thought we had lost. I was in Holland at the time, so I had to talk to his wife about what had happened, why we couldn't find him right away, and what the chances were of getting him back. Daily I briefed her on the conduct of the search, how much water area we covered, and where we were going next. She was a lovely young lady, and under any others circumstances the task would have been an enjoyable one.

Two days, four days, a week, and no luck. Finally, after about ten days we found the pilot floating in his one-man life raft, half starved but, for the ordeal he had been through, in relatively good condition. It was really a pleasure to bring good news for a change—so many other times as a squadron commander I had to make that call with the doctor and the chaplain. That was the beginning of a friendship—a relationship, I should say—that a year or so later caused a lot of unhappiness in two families and made some waves in my career pattern that were much too big and treacherous for the average professional surfer.

On one of my trips from Holland to Wheelus I decided to fly a T-33 instead of an F-100. I was taking Command and Staff School by correspondence and needed some study time, so I got a good sharp lieutenant, Dick Denay, to fly me down. I crawled in the backseat to complete another lesson or two and off we went. We cleared to Pisa, Italy. I had been studying about an hour and a half—papers all over the place—with no talking to Dick because he knew I wanted peace and quiet. Suddenly Dick broke the silence with the words, "Sir, I'm lost!" Mentally I went from desk to pilot with the speed of light. "You're what?"

"I'm lost, sir, the radio compass seems to be okay, but I'm not picking up any of the stations we usually pick up en route. The standby compass is stuck." The radio compass appeared to be working but later we found it was 90° off. We were supposed to be heading south and we were actually heading west. It was initially okay but drifted off as we flew. We were in the clouds, couldn't contact anyone, and of course didn't know the compass was off.

I suggested we maintain course and keep trying to contact a radar controller. By now my study course was put away not too neatly, hopefully to be used another day. Dick and I continued to try to contact someone—later anyone—without success. Fuel was beginning to become a problem, especially if we weren't heading toward Pisa. Finally we contacted a Canadian controller who gave us our position and a heading to the nearest base.

We began our letdown from 35,000 feet, broke out of the clouds about 9,000, and began our approach to land—at Pisa? Hell, no; at Barcelona, Spain! With the compass the way it was, by the time we could contact anyone, that was the only base we could reach. What a trip. Dick took a lot of good-natured guff over that trip, but truthfully it would have been no different if I had been up front. It was just something that happens now and then if you continue to fly airplanes.

Soesterberg rocked along pretty well for a year or so, and by the summer of 1960 I was getting good reports on us everywhere I went. The 32d Squadron had been transferred from the 36th Wing to the 86th Wing at Ramstein and we were starting our first F-102 deployment to Libya. I had just arrived at Wheelus when I got a call to return to Ramstein—the 86th Wing commander wanted to see me. I jumped in an F-102 and flew back to Germany.

The next morning we had a discussion about one of the wives in my squadron. No, it wasn't a discussion at all. The Colonel had been told about my relationship with the lieutenant's wife, and all he wanted from me was yes or no. I looked like Jackie Gleason trying to explain to Alice how he lost his salary at the race track. "Yes or no," the wing CO repeated, so I had no choice, no explanation, no nothing. "Yes," I said.

Next day the vice commander, Colonel Dave McKnight, who was a good friend, told me he had been instructed to move the ratings on my officer effectiveness report (OER) one block to the left—downgrade. I deserved at least that, but not without an explanation. The least he could do was say my base was being run in an outstanding manner (his first report said as much) but that the ratings were lowered because of a social indiscretion. I went to see the 86th Wing commander about that and told him how I felt about it. He said he could see the logic in it, but things were just not done that way. That was the end of it—or so I thought at the time.

A month or so later I had a call from General Spicer's office

(Commander 17th Air Force, and next in the chain of command). He wanted to see me. I flew down from Soesterberg and reported still in my flying suit since he suggested that it was not necessary to change. We sat down in two big chairs around a table and Spicer began to talk. He said, "Boots, I have your OER here and I don't understand this. From all the indications I have, you have been running Soesterberg like a pro. What can you tell me about this?" I asked if he had spoken to my wing commander about it. "No," he said, a little irritated, "I wanted to talk to you about it or I wouldn't have called you."

At that I told General Spicer the story and my discussion with my wing commander. Spicer puffed away on his pipe—a trademark of his—and then slowly got out of his chair. He was silent for maybe thirty seconds, then turned to me and with a trace of a grin on his face asked, "Did the lady complain?"

"No, sir," I said, "it was her husband."

"Well, you know how unreasonable they can be about little things like that. Thanks for coming down, Boots." Suddenly it was over, before I thought it had really begun.

A few weeks later a friend of mine in USAFE personnel (one more step up the chain of command) called and asked if I would like to know what General Spicer did to my OER. "Does a rat have a tail? Of course I want to know."

"Well," he said, "the general put his initials in all the highest rating boxes, then added the statement, 'Soesterberg is the toughest job in my command and Lt. Col. Blesse is my best commander.' " I loved it but didn't think for a moment that praise for the job I had done erased the social indiscretion, because it did not—nor should it have. The OER was controversial, so from that time on I was simply not considered for accelerated promotion. I would go to the primary zone (twenty-one years' service) before being considered for promotion to full colonel.

Since I had made lieutenant colonel in less than thirteen years, it was going to be a long wait. Fortunately, I didn't know all that at the time. It was quite a while before Camp New Amsterdam quieted down from that one.

I was due for reassignment in November 1960, and at the time felt as though I'd be lucky to stay that long. In early October, two and a half months after the social blunder, I had a call from the 86th Fighter Wing commander. I couldn't believe my ears! He said he didn't have the quality personnel available right now for a new 32d Squadron CO and wondered if I would stay on until next summer. I thought it over carefully, and a few days later told him I would extend until June next year. The departure conditions seemed vastly improved over that of leaving right after all the trouble, and besides, it tickled me to think how he must have agonized over his own position of having to ask me to stay. Soesterberg was history but I loved every minute of it. The job prepared me for positions of greater responsibility, I met a lot of wonderful American and Dutch people, and boy, did I learn a lot about life.

In summary, my actions socially as a commander were inexcusable and it always bothered me that my friendship with Boom Boom was forced into what appeared to be an untimely, turbulent ending. Actually, about twenty-one years later, when we were both retired major generals, I saw Boom Boom in the officers' club at Langley AFB, Virginia. He had vision problems, so I was almost within speaking range before he recognized me. I wasn't sure how he would react, but for some reason right then I felt the bad feeling between us needed to be dealt with. We looked directly at each other as I took the last few steps toward him—I stuck out my hand and said I was sorry things had to be the way they were a long time ago. He continued to look at me as though in disbelief, then put his arms around me as two misty-eyed old fighter pilots buried the hatchet and began working on a shiny new friendship.

★ ★ ★

CHAPTER 16

Pre-Vietnam Years

In June 1961 I was assigned to the Air Force Inspection and Safety Center in San Bernardino, California. At one time or another over the next four years there I flew the F-100, F-104, F-4, and F-102. In addition to that I saw a lot of Christine, who had recently divorced and was working in South Gate, on the outskirts of Los Angeles.

General Jay T. Robbins was the head of the safety center while I was there. With twenty-two victories in the Pacific, he was one of the leading aces of World War II. I was delighted every time I got invited to play golf with him. Eventually Colonel Art Jeffrey, another World War II ace, and Major Gus Sonnenberg, former test pilot, and I had a weekly game with the general.

I don't know how the foursome ever stayed together, because at least once a week Jeff would back off from a putt and want to know if I was through moving around or something. General Robbins was fun to play with, but he hated to lose. When he won, we all stopped for a drink afterward; but when he lost, he would hand me twenty dollars and rush off to a meeting he had just conjured up. I paid all his debts and then reported in Monday morning to give him change and an accounting of who got what and why. Gus was the lowest ranking of the group but that didn't bother him; I had to continually remind him the general officer in the foursome was named Robbins, not Sonnenberg. I had as many hang-ups as the rest, I just didn't have enough rank to show them. It's hard to believe we all ended up lifelong friends.

I saw Christine every time I went to the Los Angeles area, which was at least once a week and sometimes more often. I guess our relationship just wasn't destined to go further; the timing was wrong. I had kids ranging from three to nine, and any serious consideration always boiled down to too many people getting hurt. "No Guts, No Glory" didn't seem to apply when it was at the expense of so many others. We saw each other often while I was in San Bernardino, and the time I was able to spend with her was very special—just as she was very special. Looking back on it, things seems to have changed for Christine and me about then, although I never blamed her. It was my own fault—my indecision and my unwillingness to make the break were not fair to her.

The four years at the safety center raced by, and before I knew it, General Robbins was telling me what a great opportunity it was to be going to the National War College. Although I had advance information, I got my official orders in the fall of 1964 to attend war college at Fort McNair in Washington, D.C. The school year was August 1965 to August 1966 and that was a busy time. I played on the softball, volleyball, squash, and handball teams and spent what little time I had left writing my thesis. I elected to take the master's degree course from George Washington University, requiring a class a week during the school year and an extra month or so after graduation.

I was proud of my effort on the thesis—out of 140 papers from Army, Navy, Air Force, Marine, and State Department personnel, it was selected as one of the five best. I also wrote a paper on how to win in Vietnam, which the school requested. In 1965–66 the country was asking for answers to our involvement in Southeast Asia. I completed a paper which, as my thesis on the Cuban Missile Crisis, had to be presented to the entire class. The State Department attendees were not my strongest supporters, but that was okay; I didn't think much of the weak-sister solutions they came up with, either.

Before I knew it, the year was over and assignments were trickling in. It looked like I was going to long-range plans in the Pentagon but I had other ideas. I volunteered for service in Vietnam and that took priority. When I had successfully finished the extra month of study to get my master's degree in International Relations, I was assigned to the F-4 transition course at Davis-Monthan Air Base in Tucson, Arizona. I had a lot of company. Lee Smith, John Bartholf, Chappie James, Robin Olds, and a host of others I had known in the fighter community through the years were either in the course or were taking a refresher en route to Vietnam.

In the fall of 1966, during the F-4 course, I got promoted to colonel and that had a direct influence on what came later. My assignment as a squadron commander in the Eighth Wing at Ubon, Thailand, was cancelled and for several months I didn't know where I was going. Robin Olds and Chappie James were on the way to Ubon. Chappie wanted me to be his assistant director of operations, but I wasn't too keen about that. I flew F-51s with Chappie in Korea and, although I liked him, I didn't want to work for him. The same was true with Robin Olds. He was a strong, forceful leader, but he was a World War II ace and I was a Korean ace. I couldn't see that he needed me or that my ideas would have much effect on his operation.

I chose instead to go to Da Nang Air Base in South Vietnam. Neither the commander nor vice commander were flying on a regular basis. The director of operations had been relieved and the assistant D/O was a former B-66 pilot who checked out in the F-4 right there at Da Nang. He was trying, but it's hard to get a complete education overnight. Now there was a place I could be useful. Rocket attacks notwithstanding—Da Nang, here I come!

I had a chance to see what I had selected while I was still at Davis-Monthan. One morning I got a call from operations wanting to know if I would ferry an F-4 to Vietnam. I thought that sounded great, and so did John Bartholf, who was going through the course with me. John and I had known each other since West Point. His sister was engaged to a pilot who was my best friend back in the days when I lived in the Philippines, so the thought of us having our own private two-man Air Force to fly to Vietnam seemed fantastic. We both accepted with the speed of light.

We were flown to MacDill AFB in Tampa, Florida, and each assigned an F-4. Two days and a couple of test flights later we took off for Sacramento, California, where we were to join a SAC KC-135 that was to make the flight with us. It seemed like a good idea to be sure the air-refueling system in both types of aircraft were operational, so we spent a couple of days flying locally around Sacramento, making hookups and getting used to the way the SAC crews operated. When we were satisfied, we set a takeoff time and leaped off for Hawaii just like we knew what we were doing.

It was about five hours to Hickam Air Base in Hawaii, and after two refuelings and a bit of bad weather we were glad to see the little dot in the Pacific appear on the horizon. We were delayed three or four days in Hawaii because of bad weather, and during that time I ran into Kay—the love of my life from the Philippines in 1939. I had not seen her since the day she got married at the Fort Myer, Virginia, chapel just before I went to West Point. Her husband was an Air Force two-star general in logistics, settled in life in a nice home in Hawaii. He didn't seem that much older than I, but here I was a full colonel flying fighters and preparing to go off to war again. I couldn't help thinking she probably got the better end of the deal.

A day or so later we took off for Guam. The flights were getting longer and it seemed like my bladder was getting smaller. You haven't lived until you have tried to urinate into a small conical-shaped device, designed to overflow at the slightest sign of any real relief. Keeping the aircraft straight and level at the same time was a trick worthy of Houdini's attention. I was constantly hungry but afraid to eat for fear my bowels would mistake me for a normal person. I was drowsy, but there was no relief from that, either. I kept telling myself how great this was, flying halfway around the world in your own private jet—and in spite of everything, it really was.

After almost nine hours we arrived at Guam and had to shoot a ground-controlled approach in the rain to land. From there, after a good night's sleep, we refueled our last time over the Philippines, and flew directly to South Vietnam, landing at Da Nang Air Base.

I hadn't been on the ground an hour when I found myself in the middle of a rocket attack. The North Vietnamese had snuck into an area close to the base and let eight or ten rockets go. It wasn't too bad, except you never knew how many were coming or where the next one would hit. One rocket can be a big attack if it hits on or near your own living quarters. It seemed like a big event that night, but looking back, it was relatively minor. During the next year, I was to see some *real* rocket attacks.

John continued on to Ubon in Thailand to deliver his F-4, and a couple of days later we met as planned in Bangkok. No one knew exactly where we were, and flights to the U.S. were frequently delayed or cancelled, so John and I decided we would have ourselves a little vacation in Bangkok. We shopped, did some sight-seeing, played golf, and just enjoyed ourselves tremendously. There were a million little sidewalk shops and eating places plus the usual Air Force billets that all had nice restaurants. A week or ten days later, when the Bangkok memories exceeded those of trying to pee into that devilish little conical device, we decided to return to Tucson. It was a once-in-a-lifetime adventure, like taking a raft down the Mississippi River all by yourself.

We weren't home more than a week or so when my orders came in officially. The family stayed in Tucson and I was off to Da Nang for a year—a year of frustration, anxiety, tension, enjoyment, gratification, sadness, and, yes, fear. I always felt fear was normal, nothing to be ashamed of as long as you didn't allow it to effect the way you did your job. But that wasn't always easy.

★ ★ ★

CHAPTER 17

The Da Nang Gunfighters

Da Nang was a mess. We shared operational use of the base with the Vietnamese, and neither the previous American commander nor Vietnamese commander appeared to have a handle on the wide variety of problems that faced them. Quarters were dirty and supplies were left unprotected. The clubs, though available, were not well run, and to make matters worse, the senior officers in the wing were doing little or no flying.

In the F-4 operational world, we had a little of everything at Da Nang. We had a night mission in North Vietnam, close support for the Army in South Vietnam, we had missions in Laos, and finally we had the mission to strike targets deep in North Vietnam, mainly in the Hanoi area.

The first person to meet me when I arrived was my National War College classmate, Bert Brennan, and he laid this all out to me in a couple of hours. The wing commander had been relieved but the next assigned commander wasn't to arrive for several months. Therefore a temporary commander, Brigadier General selectee Jonsey Bolt, had been assigned from Seventh Air Force Headquarters in Saigon. The wing's vice commander was leaving, so Colonel Cliff Myers moved in to take his spot.

Bert and I discussed all these things in the DOOM (Da Nang

Officers Open Mess) Club that night. Since my date of rank was a month or so earlier than Bert's, I became director of operations and Bert became my assistant. This was a bad break for Bert since he was an extremely bright, capable officer and was more than ready for greater responsibility. That night in the club, Bert and I shook hands in a pledge that we would be two full colonels who flew a hundred missions "Up North." The tour of duty was one hundred missions in North Vietnam; missions in South Vietnam and Laos didn't count towards completion of your Southeast Asia tour. For "bird" colonels and above, the tour was one year regardless, so many lost the incentive to fly since they had to stay a year anyway. Bert and I decided you can't push a piece of string—hence, our pact to fly the same missions as the buck pilots. Our first move toward making Da Nang a respectable combat outfit was to schedule ourselves into "Pack Six" with the others.

North Vietnam was divided into what we called "route packages" for the purpose of scheduling. There were seven of these, but Route Package Six-A (Pack Six Able) was the USAF Hanoi mission. You wrote home the night before you flew there.

There was much to do when I arrived. Bert, John Bartholf, Lee Smith, Norm Gaddis, Trav McNeil, and a host of others that ended up in the war zone were all in the 1965–66 class at the National War College. Bert got to Da Nang only a week or so before I, so we essentially started on the rebirth of Da Nang at the same time.

The outfit had nine major accidents the previous year, almost all the result of operations during the monsoon season. From October to March, it was not unheard of to get twelve inches of rain overnight. The dual 10,000-foot runways were high in the middle, tapering off to the sides so the water would run off. It was a great idea unless you were landing on a wet runway. At higher speeds, right after touchdown, you had good rudder and aileron control and could keep the aircraft heading straight. As speed decreased to about 60 knots, however, rudder and aileron control decreased, leaving you brakes only to control the aircraft. Braking produced skidding and loss of control, and it wasn't long before the aircraft was off the runway sans landing gear. Somehow we had to solve that problem.

Other problems also needed attention. We were averaging thirty-five to forty hits a month in the traffic pattern, as Vietcong took potshots at landing aircraft. Operations directives for checkout and general operation were nonexistent or inadequate. Morale was not good because senior officers didn't fly much and living quarters were poor. The base was frequently rocketed at night. There was inadequate transportation on the flight line. There were no athletic facilities whatsoever except an open handball court on the Marine side. You might say that beside those things, Da Nang was a great place to be: "Other than that, Mrs. Lincoln, how did you like the play?" We got to work.

Within the wing I had a bottomless pit filled with bright, capable, young officers all willing and eager to help out if called upon. But first things first. We solved the runway problem by getting the Marines to put in two aircraft barriers on each runway 4,000 feet from each end. From either direction, then, we had a barrier to catch us.

After Bert and I and several other pilots experimented for a while, we established the procedure everyone would use when the runway was wet. Touchdown 1,000 feet or so before the barrier, no brakes, steer the aircraft with aileron into the barrier, then clear the runway for the next aircraft. This was possible because the Air Force, when it bought the Navy F-4 Phantom, decided it was cheaper to leave the carrier tailhook on the aircraft than to remove it.

If it wasn't raining, we were practicing. We averaged about 260 "traps" (barrier engagements) a month from then on, and in the monsoon season (October to March), we had only one accident. We changed the pattern of our patrols around the field and markedly reduced the hits we received in the traffic pattern. The new vice commander, Cliff Myers, with Bert and I were all flying Up North, and Colonel Bolt also was flying on a regular basis. Things were looking up.

The wingco addressed the quarters and club problems, and Bert and I chopped away at operational deficiencies. We wrote new directives and established new procedures, but most importantly we flew—me one day, Bert the next. Soon it was time for new ideas.

I had felt for years we went the wrong direction in the Air Force when we decided guns no longer were necessary. This was "the missile era," they said. I was told by some pretty high-ranking officers I was wrong but my experience in Korea seemed to tell me otherwise. Missiles didn't always work, they had limiting parameters under which they could be fired, they were ballistic (no guidance) for several hundred feet after launch, they didn't arm immediately, and, in general, left a great deal to be desired. In addition, from an operational standpoint, you could be surprised while attacking another aircraft and find yourself in a tight turning battle. High Gs and tight turns are not ideal parameters for firing a missile, and besides, range between aircraft decreases rapidly under those conditions and you could easily find the gun a far more useful weapon. An internal gun also provides a capability at all times for targets of opportunity on the ground. For all these reasons, I found the missile and gun complementary weapons, not weapons that were in competition with each other.

The F-4C, with which we were equipped, had no internal gun, but we did have an external pod with a Gatling gun in it that could be slung underneath like a bomb or fuel tank. I thought we could take that SUU-16 gun to Hanoi and increase our air-to-air capability. I needed a weapons section in the wing to run tests to determine if this was a dumb idea or a good one. Lieutenant Colonel Fred Haeffner, Majors Jerry Robbinette, Ed Lipsey, Bob Dilger, Sam Baake, Captains Bob Novak, Skip Cox, Jim Craig, and others all earned their pay and then some experimenting with the gun and other problems such as munitions loads, barrier procedures, chaff drops, drag chute procedures, electronic counter-measure devices (ECM), bombing procedures, and air-to-air fighting procedures.

I needed permission from General William Momyer, 7th AF commander, to take the gun Up North, so we began a series of tests at Da Nang that would either kill the idea or give us enough data to go see him. We flew two F-4s together, one with the SUU-16 pod in the center-line position and one without. That told us the fuel to carry the pod was not excessive, especially if we let only the leaders carry it. The wingman always used a little more fuel anyway, because to stay with the leader he made more throttle changes. We turned, dived, climbed—no problems. It was a good idea, we were now sure of it.

The MiG-17s and MiG-21s were light, relatively short-range aircraft which could turn far better than our heavy F-4 that had just been aerial-refueled before our dash in over North Vietnam. The slower MiG-17s quickly learned of our poor maneuverability and established the procedure of using the tight turn as a defensive haven. We had no gun and couldn't turn with them, so unless we could get a long-range missile shot, they were quite safe. At low altitude the missiles had little success. We needed the gun to be able to take that shot at them and break up their defensive haven.

Once we had established the idea as workable, we faced another hurdle. There was no computing gunsight on the F-4C. After the extremely capable A-1C radar computing gunsight we used fifteen years earlier in Korea, it was difficult to understand how we could find ourselves in this situation. Fuzzy thinkers were sure guns no longer were useful in combat, and in some cases even had them removed from the aircraft and destroyed.

It was a disease. They pulled guns out of the F-84F and F-104 to name a couple, and—what was worse—left them out of new aircraft in the design stage. Without guns, who needs a gunsight—and that's how our predicament came about. But we decided we could make do with the fixed sight that was installed. With no lead computed, it was useless to put the pipper (aiming dot) on the enemy aircraft, because the rounds fired would all end up behind the target. The new Gatling-type General Electric 20mm gun we carried had a very high rate of fire. So high, in fact, that the rounds that came out of this single gun would strike the aircraft only about eight inches apart at 2,000-feet range. We figured if you put the pipper on the target, then moved it forward about twice as far as you thought necessary before you began to fire, you would over-lead the target. The procedure then was to begin firing as you gradually decreased your amount of lead. This would allow the enemy aircraft to fly through your very concentrated burst. Wherever hits occurred, the rounds stitched through the wing or cockpit area like a sewing machine. Clusters of 20mm rounds striking close together would weaken the wing or what-ever it hit, and the violent air and G forces would tear it off the aircraft.

Next we put two guns on the outboard wing stations and tested that setup for destroying ground targets. Then it was three guns—two outboard and one on the centerline. All worked perfectly and each had its own usefulness, depending on the target and how far away it was. Three guns if it was close to base, two guns and an extra fuel tank if it was farther away. It was time to brief General Momyer. We were ready to use the gun in combat.

With my wing commander's approval, I got on Momyer's schedule, jumped in an F-4, and headed for Saigon. Charts and all, I parked myself in the general's outer office and awaited my turn. Finally the door opened and "Spike" Momyer ap-peared. With him was Colonel Robin Olds, commander of the 8th Tac Fighter Wing at Ubon. His outfit had been flying escort for the F-105s and F-4s that were bombing targets in Route Pack Six. Our outfit, the 366th TFW, had been doing all air-to-ground work until two weeks before, when we were sud-denly brought into the air-to-air mission. General Momyer, seeing me waiting and remembering the subject, turned to Robin Olds and invited him to hear my briefing.

So, with my select audience of two, I laid out our ideas, our test results, our method of compensating for the lack of a computing gunsight, and our ideas for air-to-ground use of the gun. It was magnificent, I thought—innovative, thorough, concise. I was quite happy with myself as General Momyer reflectively turned to Colonel Olds and said, "What do you think of that idea, Robin?"

Olds then proceeded to blow me out of the water, hull and all, with the simple statement, "General, I wouldn't touch that with a ten-foot pole!" My first thought was that killing was too humane. He didn't have to launch me to the moon with no escape hatch. I was stunned. General Momyer was more kind. "You and I talked about this a few years ago, Boots, and I didn't think much of the idea then. Maybe things are a little different now, I'm not sure. I think you have a hole in your head, but go ahead with your gun project and keep me informed."

It wasn't the wholehearted support I was shooting for, but at least we could go on with it. I couldn't believe what Robin did to me. He was a very senior colonel and I a very junior one, but we had crossed paths before. His brother was a West Point classmate of mine. We had both been in the fighter business some twenty-two to twenty-five years, and I guess I expected something softer. Robin was normally about as subtle as a kick in the ass, so my expectations weren't very realistic. I liked him, though. He was a hell of a fighter pilot and a great leader of men as long as he was in combat when the lines of supervision were not drawn too tight.

At Da Nang my weapons section continued its sterling work, and around the first week in May 1967, Major Bob Dilger and I flew the first gun-equipped Phantoms into Pack Six. We were on an escort mission, dying to try out our new toy, so when the strike forces left we hung around another ten minutes or so, hoping to see enemy aircraft. We had a couple of SAMs (surface-to-air missiles) fired at us and decided being there alone wasn't too brilliant. The next day we tried it again—same results, but no SAMs.

Colonel Bolt, the 366th Wing commander, dropped over to see me after we landed and were back in operations. "We have several other missions besides the Hanoi run and I expect you to be active in them all. You can't be going to Pack Six every day, so get back to spreading yourself around." He mentioned he was going to Hong Kong for four days. The next day we had two flights with guns on the leader and element leader's aircraft.

It was late in the afternoon when the first F-4s began returning from Pack Six. A couple of pilots oozed out of their cockpits in sweat-drenched flight suits and began to tell their story.

"Wall-to-wall MiGs, Colonel. You should have been there!"

I already knew that. As the other pilots drifted in, the story became more clear. We had nailed three MiGs—two of them with the gun. Captains Hargrove and Craig got the gun kills. It was a great day and, though I would like to have gotten one myself, I was so proud of what these guys had done I couldn't sleep that night. But in all honesty, there was another reason I couldn't sleep.

With the wing commander in Hong Kong, I had to write the daily operational summary that went to General Momyer when everything was back on the ground. I mentioned all our air-to-ground strikes in support of the Army, some attacks in the lower part of North Vietnam, and then got around to the air war.

"We engaged enemy aircraft in the Hanoi area, shooting down three without the loss of any F-4s. One was destroyed with missiles, an AIM-7 that missed and an AIM-9 heat-seeker that hit. That kill cost the U.S. government $46,000. The other two aircraft were destroyed using the 20mm cannon—226 rounds in one case and 110 rounds in the other. Those two kills cost the U.S. government $1,130 and $550, respectively. As a result of today's action, it is my personal opinion there will be two pilot's meetings in the theater tonight—one in Hanoi and the other at the 8th TFW at Ubon.'' I reread the wire, laughed my ass off, and fired the message off to 7th AF Headquarters.

Within an hour someone had called Robin and read him the wire. He used the phone to call me from Thailand, but I don't think he needed it.

"What the hell are you trying to do, you crazy bastard! Don't you realize what kind of a position this puts me in?'' He raved on until finally I said, "Wait a minute, Robin. You wanted consideration from me in this wire? Where was your consideration for me when General Momyer asked what you thought of my idea? You dug your hole and now that you're barely able to peek out of it, you can get out any way you can.'' He hung up and I had the sensation he was not happy.

A couple of weeks later I took an F-4 into Ubon because our weather was below minimums. As I sat on a barstool in the club, I saw Robin come through the door—almost literally. He came directly for me and something told me I may need the stool I was sitting on. He got about ten feet from me, broke into a broad grin, and stuck out his hand. As I shook hands with him, he said, ''It's been a long time since I had my ass chewed out by a junior colonel.'' That was Robin. That was the reason his troops loved him and would go to hell and back with him. He was controversial, but more important, he was unquestionably one of the most effective wing commanders in Southeast Asia. Robin was, and is, something else.

When I first got to Da Nang, the 366th's mission was, and had been for some time, strictly air-to-ground. Early in the war our wing had gotten some aerial victories, but those people were long gone. In fact, when I arrived in April 1967, there wasn't anyone in the outfit who had ever fought an enemy aircraft except me. It was therefore with some mixed emotions I read the wire from 7th Air Force assigning us to escort duty for the F-105s and other F-4s, along with Robin's 8th TFW. It had been twelve years since I wrote the tactics manual *No Guts, No Glory*, and fifteen since the last of my dogfighting days in Korea. But that seemed a logical place to start, so I called together the squadron that was next in Pack Six, and we began briefing air-to-air tactics out of *No Guts, No Glory*.

I told the aircrews we were using fifteen-year-old information, but it worked last time and so we would pick it up from there. I'd talk with them and at the end of the day we would modify for tomorrow what seemed outdated. In actual practice this worked well, and after some additions rather than changes, we began giving the 8th TFW a run for its money.

Our air-to-air war only lasted about six weeks but we bagged eleven MiGs in that time—more than any wing in Southeast Asia. We bet Robin's gang we would overtake them in total kills by the end of July 1967, but we were needed again in our strike capacity, and air-to-air combat became a thing of the past for us. I was really proud of the guys during that period—they did good work.

One thing that really irritated me was the newspaper coverage of our wing. After a big mission, the coverage was usually about the "Wolfpack" of the 8th TFW with a casual mention of kills "by the 366th TFW." We had no nickname—nothing catchy for the press to refer to, nor did we have a representative insignia. I decided to change all that. One morning I got the weapons section and the squadron commanders together to discuss the problem of our lackluster appearance. After a three-minute discussion, I told them all to go to the head because, when they got back, no one was going to leave the room till we had a new insignia and a new name.

It worked. After a half-dozen or so half-assed ideas, some-one came up with the name "Gunslingers." It was close but it still needed something. Finally one of the guys blurted out, "I've got it! How about The Gunfighters—The Gunfighters of Da Nang?" It was perfect. We had done all this testing on the gun and had gotten the first kills with it, so what name could be better?

At that moment Major Ed Lipsey spoke up. "I have just the thing for our new insignia." He then left the room to return with a large maintenance manual. On one of the armament pages was a picture of McDonnell Douglas's cartoon Phantom, which was the name of the F-4. It was ideal; a funny little guy in a black full-length coat wearing tennis shoes and a very large black hat, carrying a SUU-16 gun pod. He had the pod against his hip as though he was about to spray the area with 20mm rounds.

The rest was easy. We had several pilots who were artists in their own right, so I gave each of them the ingredients and asked for some sketches the next day. A few changes in color and wording and we had a nickname, a patch, and a wing full of people enthralled with the idea of being "The Gunfighters of Da Nang." It did have a nice ring to it. We had patches made for our flight suits, plaques for departing pilots, and we originated the Gunfighter Stagecoach that traveled the flight line twenty-four hours a day. Additionally, a company in the States run by a man who lost his son in Vietnam gave us about sixty adhesive decals three feet by four feet in size. On our aircraft they looked beautiful. Every day it was a new wrinkle as someone came up with something innovative. The only thing that mattered was that we successfully changed our image in our own eyes and of those around us. After 1 May 1967 when this all happened, we were always referred to in "the dispatches" as "The Gunfighters of Da Nang."

Before our period in the air-to-air war came to a close we had some untimely occurrences. A midair collision near Hanoi sent my second GIB (Guy in Back), Ron Webb, to a POW camp for the rest of the war. I wasn't flying that day and he was scheduled with one of our operations officers. I went through five F-4s during my 157 missions, and I was only flying every other day. Everyone had their share of SAM firings and AAA hits.

I would like to have scored a victory or two, but it was not to be. You didn't see enemy aircraft too often, and when you did, things had to be right. My big moment came early in May while we were giving top cover to some F-105s striking the Hanoi area. As we were making a sweep around Hanoi above the bombers, a surface-to-air missile (SAM) headed directly for my flight. As we steepened our turn, the missile—which always looked the size of a telephone pole—came through the area and exploded just beyond me and underneath my wingman. I couldn't believe I wasn't hit because the explosion rocked my aircraft but the blast pattern was away from me. My wingman reported calmly and succinctly, "Shit, I'm full of holes!" As soon as I was sure he meant the aircraft and not himself, I gave him a heading west toward the tanker tracks. He was streaming a little of everything and the aircraft looked like it had been hit by about forty shotguns from twenty feet. I hoped he could get out of the Hanoi area before he had to eject.

As my wingman took up a heading toward the west tanker tracks, I became his eyes and his lifeline—watching for MiGs, other SAMs, and avoiding the heavier flak areas. We were between the Red and Black rivers west of Hanoi, heading out of the area, when I spotted two MiG-21s chasing some F-105s about 10,000 feet below us. I watched them for several minutes heading west like we were, totally unaware of us. Finally, convinced they were not going to catch the F-105s, they made a gradual sweeping turn to the south, then back eastward to Hanoi. I have seen those two MiG-21s turn their tails to me a hundred times in my sleep. I needed thirty, maybe forty-five seconds, to dive, line up, and fire a couple of missiles from low at six o'clock where they usually work. But the two kills would have meant nothing if I had lost my wingman—it just wasn't meant to be.

We continued across the Black River and on into Laos where we contacted our assigned tanker. That ole F-4 continued to fly regardless of the fluids streaming from it, and except for having to take on extra fuel, my wingman made it all the way back to Da Nang without further trouble. We counted 164 holes in his

Phantom when it was all over. My air-to-air war was over, too. That turned out to be my last chance to shoot down an enemy aircraft.

In May 1967, 7th Air Force put out a memorandum suggesting an exchange of information between the various fighter wings in the theater. It would be accomplished by each wing's director of operations flying with other wings to see how they accomplished their combat mission. Early that month Colonel Norm Gaddis, D/O at Cam Ranh Bay, came to fly with us for a week. He flew our South Vietnam mission in support of the Army, and several missions in Laos and the southern portion of North Vietnam.

Before he left, Norm wanted to go on one of our Hanoi strikes since his wing was not assigned any missions in Pack Six. The request was approved, and it was decided he would fly my wing on the afternoon mission the next day.

Pack Six was different from all the other missions we flew in Vietnam. You knew ahead of time you were going to have plenty of ground fire and antiaircraft artillery (AAA). You would possibly get a few SAMs fired your way, and there was the possibility you would be jumped by MiGs while you were loaded with bombs on the way in. The MiGs didn't stay to fight—they came up the back of the formation, one or two at a time, fired a couple of missiles, and climbed out of sight. It was always interesting and a bit hairy.

The real threat was groundfire. Out of a sixteen-ship strike force, five or six would usually come back with holes and frequently one or two wouldn't get back at all. I flew every other day for a year, and in that time we lost thirty-nine aircraft. That meant seventy-eight guys used the ejection seat and were in enemy territory from two hours to seven years, depending on where they went down.

We had helicopters and A-1s on call twenty-four hours a day—the Jolly Green Giants and the Sandys—who went into hostile areas under conditions you wouldn't believe. If a shootdown was too far away for rescue aircraft, some radar operator would vector other fighters to the area and get them to establish contact with the downed crews. We all carried survival radios that allowed us to talk to airborne aircraft in the event we went down.

About 1400 hours on the day of the mission, Norm and I and the others briefed, headed out to our aircraft, and began the long procedure to provide cover for F-4s and F-105s who were going to upset Charlie's rice bucket Up North. Missile and armament checks on the ground were performed in a designated area, and while we were working to have all the safety pins removed and fuses armed, you could look fifty feet across the ramp at a Pan Am jet full of normal people staring out the window at you. An occasional thumbs-up made you proud to be a fighter pilot. Da Nang continued to operate as a civilian airport during all but the most desperate times, so Pan Am and others usually were there.

We got airborne, joined up, and headed for the refueling track, which today was on the west side out over the mountains in Laos. I never flew a mission into Pack Six without feeling intense pride in the whole Air Force operation. EB-66s blanked enemy radar scopes, the Jollys and Sandys were on call if we needed them, and the KC-135 tankers were in position waiting to give thirsty fighters a burst of energy that would propel them into areas only a fool would attempt to penetrate. Yet we did it day after day regardless of SAMs, AAA, MiGs, losses, weather, or anything else. Right, wrong, or indifferent, it was a magnificent operation. Consider the cooperation between the different elements of the strike force—the fighters, the tankers, the rescue people, the Iron Hand flights who struck enemy defenses before we got there, and the Wild Weasels who took on the missile sites with their antiradiation missiles, and, of course, the strike pilots who dove through it all to put the bombs where they were told to put them. After we stirred 'em up good, we called the RF-4s to come in and take pictures of what we had done. It was a sea of harmony and cooperation that gave me goose bumps on more than one occasion.

It was with these thoughts in mind that we took on our fuel and accomplished our final checks before heading into Pack Six. Coming off the tanker, I was making my final checks and found that I couldn't arm my missiles. We were protecting the fighter-bombers on this mission, which made me useless, so after several more unproductive tries I decided I had to abort. The strike force went northeast and I went southeast.

I was furious. I had left Norm in a three-ship flight, which I didn't like; I just wanted to be there. I flew on a few minutes and, in a fit of anger, I hit the armament switch with my hand as I had done ten times before, and for some reason everything came back on line. I made a quick call to the strike leader to tell him I was cutting across the southern part of Pack Six in an attempt to rejoin my flight. That was okay, and in a few minutes I spotted the three-ship flight and rejoined. Soon we were in the Hanoi area providing cover for F-105s and F-4s striking targets just west of town. A SAM was fired at us, beginning a sequence of events that was not to end until nightfall. When a SAM was fired in our area, it was our procedure to turn, placing the missile at either 90° left or right (at three or nine o'clock) to judge its approach.

The SAM usually went above you and descended—from there you could determine if it was guiding toward you. If so, you took your flight down as steeply as possible, watching the missile increase its dive angle. At the last moment you would pull up, and the SAM, unable to turn as tight, would fly into the ground. It required good timing and calm heads, but it worked.

That day west of Hanoi, the missile had our name on it, so over we went. When we had pulled up and stabilized, there was another SAM call and an enemy aircraft "heads up" call after which I couldn't get a response from Norm. We circled an airfield called Hoa Lac, twisting, turning, looking for any signs of him. Suddenly, we saw a single Phantom about 15,000 feet below, going very slow with a MiG behind him. Before we could reach the F-4, the MiG hit him with cannon fire and

Norm and his backseater ejected. We saw one chute and people on the ground picking up the pilot immediately. During our next circle of the field, we began drawing heavy AAA fire and climbed away.

It was over two years before we found out Norm was alive. The North Vietnamese reported him dead, showing his flight-suit name tag on TV, and kept him isolated for several years. During a transfer to another camp, a friend spotted him and the word soon got back to the States that he was alive.

The mission seemed over and the remaining three of us headed back to the tanker, wondering what really happened to Norm and his backseater.

Before we could get refueled, we had a call from the radar director ship "Red Crown," telling us of a downed F-105 pilot. We were to return and attempt to make contact with him. We took on some fuel and headed back into Pack Six with the coordinates of the downed pilot. Though we circled at low altitude, making numerous calls, we got nothing but ground-fire.

We assumed, if we were at the right spot, the Thud pilot was afraid to use his radio because of enemy activity. After thirty minutes or so we went to the tanker again, got more fuel, and returned to try again. We heard a call or two from the '105 driver, but never got an answer when we responded.

Finally, with the shadows creeping across the hillside and fuel again becoming a problem, we headed to the tanker for the last time. It was now obvious that it would be dark when we got back to Da Nang. My pressurization system failed, and suddenly I found myself having to choose between fuel and no oxygen or oxygen and no fuel. I tried a compromise at about 12,000 feet—any lower and I wouldn't have fuel enough to make it.

Fortunately, Da Nang's weather was good. But as I began my letdown, descending in the dark, my canopy began to fog up. I couldn't see out, so I contacted GCA and had them bring me in. Even at 200 feet I couldn't see the runway on the first pass so they took me around again. I had fuel enough for just one more attempt and GCA gave me a safe-ejection-area-heading, just in case.

Well into the final approach my windscreen began to clear a little and that was all I needed. Feeling that F-4 back on the runway was a sensation second to only one thing, and that hadn't crossed my mind all afternoon. I taxied into the dearming area to drop my drag chute and suddenly the effect of the mission hit me. I had refueled four times on that seven-hour flight. We were unable to locate the F-105 pilot and then, when I got back, I had to shoot two night GCAs wondering if I was going to land or bail out. But more devastating than all of that, we had lost Norm and his GIB. It all rushed through me in a wave of frustration, fatigue, anger, and sadness, and the next thing I knew I was sitting in that dark cockpit with my oxygen mask off and tears streaming down my face. The crew chief climbed up on the aircraft, took one look at me, and I heard, "Christ, Colonel, are you okay?"

"Yeah, I'm okay," I blubbered, "kind of a rough day at the office."

The next time I saw Norm was in Hawaii six years later when he came back with the returning POWs. We hugged, had a rather tearful reunion, and then filled each other in on the details of that fateful day in May 1967. Great fighter pilot—great guy. They don't come much better than ole Norm Gaddis.

Not long after Norm was shot down our new commander, Colonel Bob Maloy, arrived on the scene. Good or bad, the presence of a permanently assigned commander has a stabilizing influence on an outfit. Bob Maloy was exactly what we needed. He knew lots of people in places where it counted, he was a good, experienced fighter pilot, and he was a leader who never forgot for one moment that his NCOs were the backbone of the outfit. The base began to reflect his presence almost immediately. He was usually up at the crack of dawn, driving around looking for things that needed to be done. He carried a small tape recorder with him, and after his morning tour he would deposit the tape on his secretary's desk. By ten-thirty, people were reading both the problem and what he wanted done about it. He did more before ten o'clock each day than most commanders accomplish in a week, and he did it in a businesslike but pleasant way that made people want to do better. He flew his share, especially when you consider the enormity of the job he had. I liked the way he chose his missions by day and time, long before anyone knew what the target would actually be. No matter how tough the mission, he always flew it. Sometimes after a really rough one, he would catch me in the club and with a twinkle in his eye, he'd say, "Hey, Slippery, you tryin' to move up a notch or somethin'?"

I really enjoyed working for Bob, he was a top-notch commander in every way. He left operations to me, even allowing me the privilege of decorating those officers who had distinguished themselves in combat. I had a personally designed ceremony for those special moments, because it gave me a great sense of pride to pin a medal on a pilot who had "hung it out" to accomplish a difficult mission for the outfit and for his country. Colonel Maloy would agree occasionally to come over to present a Silver Star or a medal for unusual valor during a rocket attack or something like that, but generally he preferred to remain on top of things and let me handle the pilots.

Rocket attacks at Da Nang were something you just learned to live with. It was never a big deal unless the rocket hit in your area, but that was the thing about them—even the North Vietnamese who fired them didn't know where they would land. The chance always existed that the next one would have your name on it. We increased base security, watched for infiltrators from low-flying aircraft, and had patrols in the most logical areas. Nothing helped too much. The little black-suited guys would creep in, set up a crude launcher for their 140mm rockets, launch eight or ten in a 60-second period, and disappear into the night. We lost some aircraft, some buildings, and some people, but considering the size of our operation, most attacks would have to be classified as a nuisance.

However, the attack on the night of 14 July 1967 was almost catastrophic. It began just before midnight and continued for about a half hour. When it was over, we had lost about eighteen of the 390th Squadron's complement of F-4 aircraft, several C-123 and C-130 cargo planes, had many buildings destroyed, and suffered numerous casualties. If the midnight shift had not been late that night to the flight line, we would have lost a couple hundred airmen along with all those aircraft. One runway had eight or nine large holes that rendered it useless for a while, but the other was okay. With the aircraft that were flown in to us early the next day, we were back in operation by noon.

When the attack began my roommate Bert Brennan and I were sound asleep. We pulled on some trousers and shoes and dashed for the nearest bomb shelter. From a slit in the shelter door I watched the ammunition dump on the Marine side take a direct hit. It looked much like a mushroom cloud from an atomic explosion. While I was watching the smoke, unaware of the shock wave that had been created, my hat was suddenly blown about thirty feet to the back of the revetment. It rocked the whole base. Three or four minutes later, Bert and I decided we should go down to the flight line and see how everyone was making out. We dashed for our jeep and began to negotiate the winding one-mile road. Fires were everywhere, with aircraft burning all over the place, but there were no people. They were all under cover.

Suddenly, we came on an F-4 burning in a revetment. Fuel was leaking out of the Phantom into the next parking place toward another F-4 on alert. The alert aircraft was fully loaded with eight 750-pound bombs; if that burned and exploded, no one we knew would live to tell about it. Bert and I sped off in the jeep and found four or five armorers who knew a lot more about disarming fuses and removing bombs than we did. We returned to the aircraft and, in the light of the fire from the next hardstand, with an occasional rocket still coming in, the six of us unloaded that F-4 and then cleared the hell out of there as fast as our lucky little asses would go.

The next morning, the seriousness of that attack became more obvious. There were some holes in both runways, aircraft were still smoldering in the hardstands and on the parking ramp, pieces of jagged, twisted metal were everywhere, and, when I got to my own aircraft, I got the shock of my life. My F-4 was perched precariously on top of the revetment in which it had been parked—upside down! The landing gear was sticking up in the air and part of one wing was missing, but otherwise it appeared to have been put up there by pranksters rather than blown up by a rocket. The revetment was a partial pyramid of sandbags, wide at the base, narrowing somewhat at the top some fifteen or twenty feet high, so whatever it was that blew that aircraft up there packed a good wallop. It felt as though I had lost a real friend and indeed I had. Less than thirty days before, she had brought me back safely after taking a direct hit from a 37mm flak gun that blew off a fuel tank and left me with a giant-size hole in the left wing. As good as she was, however, my second Phantom was history.

A couple of days later I had a call from Fred Haeffner. "Meet me down on the flight line at the south end," he said. "I have something I want you to see." God, what a sight! Sitting on the ramp was my new F-4, with "BB" on the tail just like all my others. The tail was painted with blue and white stripes and there was a big blue and white band around the fuselage. On the nose in bold white letters, it said *Blue Max*.

I would love to have kept that bird forever, but it only lasted about forty-five days. I got hit leading a flight of sixteen aircraft laying Snakeyes in a harbor in North Vietnam. Snakeyes were 500-pound bombs with fins on the back end that opened up to cause drag. That kept them behind you and allowed you to drop them at low altitude without blowing yourself up. They had proximity fuses so any boats that passed over them seldom reached their destination. I had one engine on fire, but we were so close to the drop zone I figured we might as well press on. As soon as we all had dropped our Snakes, I broke off and climbed for altitude. At about 20,000 feet, the fire went out and didn't start again until we let down near base. We alerted the crash trucks and, with one engine still on fire, landed and caught the first barrier. Needless to say, we made a hurried exit and left it for the fire crew. *Blue Max* went down the tube. It was time for another aircraft.

Flying continued at the usual rapid pace. Pilots who flew one hundred missions over North Vietnam rotated and others took their place. The squadron commanders changed and Sandy Vandenberg left.

By the end of July 1967 we were back in the air-to-ground war again. PAF (Pacific Air Forces) let us know that recent information indicated the bombing in Pack Six was not very good. Also, it was common knowledge that the last plane down the chute gets the most flak. We put those two items together and came up with what turned out to be a great idea. Why not bomb by flights, then all the aircraft would dive together and less flak would be fired at everyone. In the process only four good dive-bombers were required in a sixteen-ship strike. The rest salvoed their bombs when the leader dropped his, so we very quickly established ourselves as real pros in the dive-bombing department. It was good to know we were effective when we went to Pack Six because we really paid for it dearly. During June, we lost eleven aircraft, which means twenty-two of our pilots used the ejection seat. We got back about seven or eight but all the rest became residents of the Hanoi Hilton or were killed outright.

About this time one of the younger pilots asked if he could talk to me about a personal problem. We closed my office door and this young man laid himself bare about his fear of getting killed. I hadn't faced that problem before—most fighter pilots have a way of covering it up with overconfidence. I let him talk for at least ten minutes without interrupting him, and then told him how I felt and what I thought could be done about it. I told him he certainly wasn't the only guy in the outfit that wanted to live through this. We all felt just as he did. We all felt fear and apprehension in different degrees but, no matter what degree, we had to learn to cope with it. Fear is natural. You just have to resolve that it will not affect your performance.

I explained that we had outstanding air-rescue facilities, and that much of the time being shot down didn't mean being killed or taken prisoner. If you were prepared for it, you would probably make it okay. The risk could never be eliminated any more than it was for our pilots in World War II. In Europe they flew five hundred miles behind enemy lines with no air rescue at all, attacking airfields, depots, railroad yards, and a host of other well-defended targets. They did it regardless of risk because it was their job. In the Pacific, they flew for hours over water to finally attack a well-defended island airfield. No rescue to fall back on, just personal resolve to do the job they had been assigned. Those pilots created a heritage, a standard for us all, and we simply had no recourse but to measure up to it. I gave him a moment or two to think about that and then said, "If none of that means anything to you, or you feel you can't cope with it, then I want you to lay your wings on my desk and I'll get you transferred to a noncombat assignment."

A pilot without the will and determination to do the job very often gets killed, and in the process may cause another death because of his failure to do what others expect of him. Several years later, on a barstool in an officers' club, this same pilot thanked me for that discussion. He said it helped him to know that I was scared just like he was, and that he doubted he would have finished his tour if we hadn't sat down together that day and talked about it.

As a sidelight to this, the Air Force produced a magnificent film in 1944, narrated by a young actor named Ronald Reagan, that told the story of the 8th Air Force in Europe. It has all the best air-to-air and air-to-ground combat shots that were available at the time. I had seen it when I was a young pilot in the

56th Wing at Selfridge AFB during the late Forties. When I was commander at Soesterberg in 1959, I received a notice that *Fight for the Skies* was to be destroyed along with others no one wanted. I wrote a three-page letter explaining why they should spare *Fight for the Skies*. It was fighter-pilot history and would be needed in a thousand ways in the event of a future conflict. Fortunately, it was saved and I used it in 1967 and 1968. It was mandatory viewing for new pilots before they began their flying tour at Da Nang. It struck me as a great idea after talking to that young pilot.

Visitors—did we have visitors! We had 'em from 7th AF, from PAF, from the Pentagon, congressional staff visits—you name the organization and we had 'em as visitors. We briefed each group with the same patience and care to be sure they learned what we were contributing to the overall effort in Southeast Asia.

By August the Gunfighters were a well-oiled machine, proud of the outfit and what it could do, and they were coming up with an idea a day to make it even better. Someone saw an article in the paper about a very large insignia, 100 feet in diameter, placed on a hangar at a base in the States. I guess the guys were talking about it at the club, and the next day they approached me about putting one on the top of one of the hangars at Da Nang. It had to be at least 175 feet in diameter so it would be the largest in the USAF. Well, we took the idea to Colonel Maloy, who then suggested it to the base civil engineer. The engineers studied it, then estimated it would take seven months to do it and require more paint than was in the theater of operations. Bob Maloy said no to the project based on the civil-engineering report.

A few days later one of the squadron commanders, Lieutenant Colonel Fred Haeffner of the 390th, asked if his squadron could take it on as a project. He outlined how they planned to do it and, after checking with Maloy, I gave him the okay. The pilots in the 390th, after we sent our C-47 to a couple of bases for paint, began the project on a Friday and had it completed before Monday morning. It was a magnificent effort which made *The Stars and Stripes* and *The Air Force Times*. I think everyone loved it except the civil engineer. The CO would ask him something about it in the staff meeting once or twice a month just to needle him a little. Fred Haeffner, retired as a major general, remembers the masterpiece his squadron turned out:

"The hangar roof had rivets on it located approximately one foot apart, horizontal and vertical. We took a piece of graph paper and scaled down a drawing of the patch on the graph paper where each square, as I recall, was two or four square feet. Then we numbered the appropriate square on the roof of the hangar between the rivets as on the graph paper. Then, with a hand-held spray can, we drew the outline on the roof by the numbers on the graph paper. We then went up in a helicopter to view the outline and made a couple of minor changes. The fighter aircrew, led by Major Larry Sharp, my executive officer, got several gallons of colored paint and a compressor with a very long hose and sprayed the appropriate colors in the proper areas. As I recall, the whole project was done on the weekend with about 1/20 the amount of paint suggested by the engineers. It was 192 feet in diameter and was really an engineering marvel." And so it was—and is. The Russians are there now and probably still trying to figure out how we did it.

The summer was hot as hell. The thunderstorms made our missions more complicated, but we continued to hammer away at the Vietcong wherever we could find them. In August, four of us, each with fifty to sixty missions, decided we needed a little R&R (rest and recuperation). After careful consideration we selected Okinawa because it had a real nice eighteen-hole golf course. We tried to play thirty-six holes a day for four days but found our hands couldn't stand it. After the second day, we were using Band-Aids on half our fingers. We got through thirty-six the third day, but cut back to eighteen the last day and barely made that.

Back at Da Nang, I was on the mission schedule the next day and drew the Pack Six run. The SAMs were flying and the air was full of flak as I rolled in my target. In my state of controlled panic I couldn't help but smile under that hot oxygen mask as I thought how sore my hands were from playing golf.

The summer raced by. Fred Haeffner and a couple of others found a way to get a two-gallon container of ice cream a week. I didn't want to know how, because it made life so much more enjoyable. The club had improved tremendously. The base, although not picture perfect, was neat, clean, and a model of efficiency compared to its original condition. The mission was going smoothly with only an occasional loss in Pack Six, and it began to seem as though we had Da Nang running pretty much the way we wanted it.

Living conditions had improved. Bert and I lived in a trailer that had two bedrooms, a small kitchen, and a sitting room—it was similar to all the others in the officers' area. All the trailers had a young Vietnamese lady assigned to keep them clean and neat. These "house girls," if you like that term, in most cases were nice girls, and as you can imagine the pilots spoiled them rotten. Bert and I were no exception. Every time we went somewhere, we brought "Sunrise" something. She had a much more sophisticated name, but we couldn't pronounce it, and since she was so pretty and such a happy person, we decided to call her Sunrise. After a while the girls were like family. They knew everyone and spoke enough English to understand comfortably.

The feeling of family was a two-way street. When one of the pilots from their immediate area was shot down, they cried and carried on much as they would have for their own brother and sister. All this was fine, except in many cases it went way beyond the brother-sister relationship. It was perfectly natural, I guess, because the longer a guy is away from home the more susceptible he is to outside entertainment. Let's face it, we get horny.

That created a problem which our flight surgeon solved in

short order. In exchange for an occasional backseat combat mission, he just included the house girls in the weekly medical inspection he had to make of all the officers' club food handlers. At least you knew one day a week what was what. The next day, who knows.

CHAPTER 18

The Golden BB

As the summer of 1967 faded, so did our good luck. Beginning in November we had a series of losses that were totally different from those we had been experiencing. We all talked occasionally about getting the Golden BB—the unlucky flak hit that destroys the aircraft and crew instantly. I'm a little hazy on the actual dates and the order in which the losses occurred, but the general circumstances are as crystal clear as though it happened yesterday.

On 9 November, during a night dive-bombing mission near Mu Gia Pass in Laos, we lost an aircraft and crew. The pilot was Lieutenant Colonel John Armstrong, commander of the 480th Squadron. His backseater was Captain Lance Sijan. John was apparently killed instantly, but somehow Sijan managed to eject at the last moment. What transpired after that was almost unbelievable. Captain Sijan landed in an area full of enemy soldiers and, though he had an operational survival radio, he was not heard from for about a day and a half. Although he had a broken leg, a mashed arm, a fractured skull, and cuts all over his body, he felt his best chance was to hide until the enemy search for him cooled down.

On the second day, Sijan began to transmit when he saw some friendly aircraft overhead. Word was passed to the rescue units, and prop-driven A-1 "Sandys" soon arrived on the scene. Lance used up all his flares helping the A-1s pinpoint his position, so when a helicopter arrived, he had difficulty getting it to his exact position. Finally, when the chopper was about a hundred yards away, Sijan told the pilot to hover, saying he would come to them. With one good foot and one good arm he rolled on his back and began pushing himself backwards toward the rescue aircraft. When he was a scant twenty yards away, the chopper was hit by ground fire and had to pull out. It was dusk, so another pickup attempt could not be made till the next day. The chopper pilot at one time offered to send down two paramedics but Captain Sijan said it was too dangerous.

The next day an armada of aircraft attempted to locate Sijan again, but to no avail. It was assumed he died of his wounds overnight or was captured because he made no further radio calls. Several days later the search was called off.

In the meantime, Lance Sijan had decided he had a better chance of rescue if he got out of that immediate area. He chose an area about twenty-five miles east, across a small mountain range, and dedicated his life to making that journey. He dragged himself backwards till his hip bones protruded, pushing with one good heel and one good arm. Almost seven weeks later he was captured about twenty-three miles from where he had ejected from his F-4.

In spite of his broken leg, mangled arm, and protruding hip bones, Sijan was given no medical treatment. Because of his condition he was left in a transfer station with only one guard. He waited for the right moment and then summoned his guard as though he wanted to say one last word. As the guard bent over him, Sijan knocked him out with a karate chop. He then escaped into the jungle and traveled a mile or so before he was recaptured. Eventually he was transferred to a POW camp where he made contact with other Americans. A short time later, around the end of January 1968, he contracted pneumonia and died. Lance Sijan was awarded the Medal of Honor for his incredible courage and will to survive.

Between 9 and 20 November, we lost several other aircraft.
As in the case of Armstrong and Sijan, they were Golden BB
losses—roll into a dive, explosion, no survivors. We tried to
stop flying and investigate our procedures, but we had no proof
that anything was wrong. As we were told, sometimes you get
losses like those in combat.

Bert had the last R&R, so I decided to take a few days off
and go to Hong Kong. He kidded about passing me in total
missions, but that didn't matter; I just felt I needed a change.
On 22 November I was in Hong Kong and it was magnificent. I slept late, bargained with the merchants, and ate
in fine restaurants for four luxurious days. On the 25th I
climbed aboard the transport and headed back to Da Nang
with a doorknob in each hand, leaving heel marks all the
way.

Fred Haeffner met me, as Bert was busy in Ops. The first
news I got was that we lost a couple more aircraft and crews—
same conditions. I wanted to fly. Fred assured me that was no
problem and said he would notify my backseater, Doug Condit. It would be the midmorning mission. Fred deposited me at
my trailer and I decided to unpack everything before going to
lunch. A few minutes later Bert came in and we carried on like
I had been gone a month or so. Bert was about as fine a guy as
I have ever met. With a good sense of humor, bright and
capable, he had that rare ability to inspire others to do better
than they knew how.

"Well, Bert," I said after a couple of subjects were discussed quickly, "how many missions did you get while I was
in Hong Kong?"

"Not one damn flight," Bert said. "The boss has had a burr
under his saddle ever since you left."

I thought about that a moment and then recounted to Bert
about being on the flight schedule the next day.

"Bert, it doesn't seem fair to me to be in Hong King four
days and then come back and fly before you do. Why don't you

take the mission instead? Doug is all set up to go. I know he would enjoy going with you.''

"Hey, boss, that's great," Bert said. "I really appreciate it." And that settled it.

I left some perfume for Sunrise, and Bert and I headed over to the club for lunch. We spent half of our lives briefing each other. I flew one day and Bert flew the next, so someone always had to be brought up to date. With that kind of schedule an "average" assistant would have been a nightmare. With Bert it was just great. He could just as easily have been the boss and I his assistant except for a few weeks' difference in our promotion dates to full colonel. Bert was to be a general someday, there was no doubt about it in my mind.

The next morning things were humming along as usual when I was suddenly jolted out of my complacent mood. Bert and Doug had apparently been shot down on a mission in Laos. It was the same description we had before—right after bomb release they apparently took a direct hit and went down in a fireball. At that moment, how it happened didn't matter to me. What did matter was that Bert and Doug were down and I had given him my mission. To this day, I cannot recount these circumstances without tears welling in my eyes and thinking again the uncomfortable thought that Bert and Doug were gone as a result of my suggestion. We sent other aircraft into the area in hope of hearing one or both of them on the survival radio, but we heard nothing. For days we overflew the area hoping for some contact but it never came. Bert and Doug were not coming back, and under the circumstances, I was having a very bad time accepting that.

About a week later we were scheduled for a mission we called "Skyspot." The aircraft flew to a designated point at which they were picked up by radar. They were then vectored, heading and distance, to another point from which a countdown began. Seconds later the radar controller called for bomb release and all four aircraft would comply. This procedure was generally used during overcast conditions to keep the enemy ducking even in bad weather.

One of our four-ship flights received a hurry-up vector, and as a result were still spread out when the countdown began. Generally, the aircraft would be within a few feet of each other, but this time the third and fourth men were several hundred yards away when the command was received to release bombs. As the leader released, three and four observed the bombs go and saw one explode a few feet under the aircraft. They got the message back and we immediately grounded everything until we could determine the problem. We lost the leader and his wingman—four aircrew.

We reasoned the cause had to do with fusing, but we couldn't get anyone in higher headquarters to agree. We had to continue to carry them, but no one said they had to be armed—so we had the fuses disarmed and tried that for a while. The losses stopped. I don't know exactly who proved what about our losses. I do know we suddenly lost eight aircraft and crews to Golden BB hits, and when we disarmed all the fuses, the losses stopped. You figure it out!

Sunrise cried for weeks at the mere mention of Bert's name. The trailer seemed empty, and even though I continued to fly frequently, I couldn't shake the circumstances surrounding Bert and Doug's death.

About a month or two later, Sunrise asked if she could shower in the trailer at the end of the day. There was a spare bedroom so I saw no harm in that, and she continued to use the shower.

One day, about six weeks later, I came back to the trailer early and Sunrise was still showering. She was usually gone by the time I got back. She came out with nothing but a towel wrapped around her and stopped by my room to ask if she was in the way. God, she looked gorgeous; slim, full-breasted, beautiful in her Oriental way, with a little devilish look in her eye. I held out my hand and she came over and sat down on the bed beside me. Soon the towel was on the floor and we were in bed. For the next twenty minutes that delicate, beautiful creature made me forget the war and everything associated with it. A week later Bert's replacement arrived and that ended that.

The tactics section kept pumping out ideas: three external gun pods for strafing, and chaff in the speed-brake well to be released during a SAM break. It was a lulu and it really worked. The squadrons put up a MiG-kill board—it was a great morale builder except for the four colonels who flew in Pack Six. When we flew, everyone knew the MiGs would not be up; we were snakebit. One day I was passing the MiG board, which was eight or ten feet high, and I saw the latest addition. It was a two-foot-high board just like the big one, giving credit to each colonel for a truck, an enemy latrine, a drinking fountain, or what have you. It got so many laughs we left it up. The guys liked the fact they had done something we hadn't done, even if there was a little luck involved in it (I keep telling myself). Frankly, we liked it too. They were doing great work.

One of the hardest things to get used to in combat is the relentless way in which the total effort is maintained regardless of losses or other unforeseen circumstances. Before I could digest the loss of even one aircraft and crew, let alone eight of them, I found myself in the selection process for a new commander of the 480th TFS. Lieutenant Colonel Bob Tanguy got the job—a good pilot, good athlete, good background. He turned out to be quite a handball and racketball player as well as a good squadron CO, and we spent many an hour on the Marine side playing one game or the other.

The one court over there was half in the open, so the slightest bit of rain made it unusable for several hours. We really needed a court of our own, so I queried the squadron commanders to see if we had any officers with experience in the construction business. As it turned out, we did. Two of our pilots had worked for their fathers' construction company in the summer for several years. They felt if they had the labor and materials, they could build what I was asking for—one long two-story building with a squash court on one end and a handball/racketball court on the other. In the center was to be a second-floor tower arrangement so a person could look down and watch play in either court.

After I had asked the pilots to draw up a list of materials, I needed to know who the laborers would be. I couldn't get the airmen involved in this. The last thing we wanted was for some guy to go to the inspector general and complain about how hard he was made to work building an athletic facility. We decided it would be done by the pilots themselves, and only those who chose to volunteer. I assured them I would take my turn on the work detail and the volunteers rolled in. So many, in fact, that inexperienced labor was never a problem to us. We had two C-47s in the wing, and everywhere they went on legitimate cargo hops, we gave them a shopping list to get from the supply people at the base.

One day I had to take a C-47 to a base too small for a fighter—a meeting of some kind. I sent a couple of people to supply for parts, paint, lumber, roofing, nails, and a hundred other things we lacked, and headed off to the meeting. At the entrance to the building I was approached by a young neatly dressed major. "Sir, could I speak to you for a minute or two?" A nod of my head and his story unfolded. He was a fighter pilot, qualified in the F-4, and had been sent to this base to fill a nonflying position. "I'll do anything you ask, give me the worst job you have in the wing, but let me come fly with the Gunfighters, please?" I could see myself ten years ago doing the same thing. I was only going to be on base an hour or so. Oh, what the hell, I thought, somebody needs to help him. I turned to him and said, "Chuck, go to your billet, pack everything you have, and be in the C-47 over there when I get ready to go. Don't sign out—there will be too many questions. I'll take care of those details when I get back to Da Nang."

Forty-five minutes later I climbed aboard and sat next to the happiest major in the Air Force. The next day Major Cunningham came around to thank a colonel who had just had his ass chewed into little bits by a senior personnel officer in Saigon: "I'll make those decisions, not you. I'll decide who goes where and when, not you, and you stay out of the personnel business. You'll hear more about this before I'm through."

I hung up the phone and smiled inwardly—he didn't order Chuck back. I assigned him to one of the squadrons and told the commander to get him flying immediately. By the time I heard from 7th AF again, he had several missions and they thought he might as well stay. Major Chuck Cunningham turned out to be a fine, aggressive combat leader who was a typical Gunfighter in every sense of the word.

After a few weeks of collecting supplies, work finally began on the athletic building. On the first day, we cleared the grass and began digging the trenches for the building foundation. It was hard work, so every couple of hours a new crew would come on. The workers were all pilots and backseaters who were not on the flying schedule. Major Pat Humphrey and a young captain called the shots. The rest of us just responded with strong backs and weak minds.

Two and half months later we had the best facility in Vietnam. We decided to name it Brennan Hall after Bert, so I penned an appropriate inscription and asked one of the guys going to Hong King to have a plate made up that we could put on the building. No building at Da Nang got more use than Brennan Hall. It was used night and day by our off-duty personnel. It still stands as a tribute to a fine officer and combat pilot and also, I might add, to the spirit and aggressiveness of the Da Nang Gunfighters. I have often wondered if the Russians, who now occupy the base, use it as much as we did. It gives me a pain in the ass just to think of that.

Regardless of how we felt about things, the war went on. By mid-January 1968, it became obvious the enemy was preparing a major effort. The Tet offensive was an all-out drive by the North Vietnamese intended to defeat once and for all the U.S. and South Vietnamese forces preventing their entry into South

Vietnam. The effort was countrywide against all South Vietnamese provincial capitals, but it was obvious Khe Sanh, Quang Tri, and Hue were the major objectives. Our wing flew in support of all three cities as required by the Seventh Air Force Tactical Air Control System, but it was at Khe Sanh where the Gunfighters got the test of their lives. Even our Hanoi missions were curtailed so our aircraft could be used "in-country."

During the 77-day seige of Khe Sanh, we found ourselves providing a major portion of the four hundred daily sorties being flown to break the back of the enemy assault. We waived minimum altitudes, and were delivering napalm from 200 feet and Snakeyes from 800 feet into enemy positions not 100 yards from our own forces. Although we continuously came back with bullet-riddled F-4s, we all tipped our hats to the C-130 pilots. During the heat of the battle, they brought those four-engine supply birds right into Khe Sanh, unloaded, and took off again. They also made low-altitude drops of equipment and supplies under conditions that would make your hair stand on end. There is little doubt that without the truly heroic effort of the C-130 boys, Khe Sanh would have fallen to the enemy.

During these tense days, I lost one of my squadron commanders—not to enemy action, to rotation. His tour was complete. Bob Tanguy, the 480th commander, and I maintained our high state of physical conditioning by continuing to butt heads in the handball and racketball courts. Although I could take him in racketball, I will very reluctantly admit he had the edge in handball. I guess I thought the competition would go on forever, but the next thing I knew we were having a hundred-mission parade for Bob.

The hundred-mission parade was a ritual the guys had developed. It kind of grew like topsy. First, a fire truck drove to the aircraft to hose down the finishing pilot as he tried to get aboard the ops truck. Soon we provided a special vehicle to protect the other pilots who just wanted to get back to quarters. Next, other vehicles began to follow the fire truck and the open truck provided for the pilot. All of a sudden, it was a ten-vehicle parade with horns honking and the fire truck taking opportune moments to again hose down the guy who was finally going home. It was the final act following the last official mission.

Tanguy got cleaned up and we all went to the club. I left early because I had a lot to do the next day, including a mission to fly in the afternoon. Bob Tanguy was to board an aircraft to the States about an hour before I was to fly. He really tied one on at the club and finally staggered to his trailer about 0100. At 0730 I went to get him. A bleary-eyed squadron CO opened the door a couple of inches and fell back from the shaft of light that struck him.

"What the hell is going on," he demanded. "I'm not on any schedule today. I'm leaving at 1400."

"Up and at 'em, Tanguy," I shouted. "You have a handball game with me and it's right now."

"You're crazy as hell, Colonel. I have to get some sleep." He tried closing the door.

"Lieutenant Colonel Tanguy, if you want to go home today, get your handball stuff and get your ass out here."

I heard him stumbling around inside muttering, "Christ, I can't believe this."

Finally, with eyes looking like two piss holes in the snow, he appeared in the doorway—shoes unlaced, shirt half on and half off. Away we drove to the handball court, each bump supposedly signaling the end of Tanguy's life. We played, he lost, I loved it, and he got on his aircraft at 1400. The last words I heard from Bob Tanguy were, "You bastard!"

CHAPTER 19

Winding Down

In early March 1968, I got word I was to be assigned to Nellis AFB for the third time, as director of operations for the F-111 wing. I couldn't believe my ears. I had no desire to fly the F-111. It was a fighter, I guess, but the mission was low-altitude night, all-weather attack. Also, there was a navigator/weapons-systems operator sitting next to you. For a guy who had spent his entire life depending on his own judgment, I was now to relinquish control to an electronic black box that would allow me to fly 100 to 500 feet off the ground at night. This box told the aircraft to climb and dive—presumably at the right time—and all you had to do was sit there and pray.

I called a friend of mine, Kenny Tallman, in the colonel's assignment branch in the Pentagon to ask for help. He said this was a directed assignment from the Air Force Chief of Staff and suggested I accept it gracefully.

In the meantime, we got a new wing commander because Colonel Maloy had broken his neck when he ejected several weeks before. He was being sent back for specialized treatment in the States. I liked Bob Maloy; he was a fine commander and good friend. He helped build the Gunfighters and did as much as anyone to see that their reputation remained intact.

I had trouble with the new commander right away. He wanted to raise all the minimum altitudes we had spent a year developing, and he wanted the mural on my office wall removed. We had a lot of restrictions under which we fought the war. One week you could hit a target, the next week it was on the no-no list. If you were on a mission to Hanoi and saw a train or other target of opportunity, you had to let it go—no authorization. We had to watch the first SAM sites being built, and couldn't strike them because there might be some Russians helping to build the site. Our feeling was if you kill the site early, you'll never have to take on more than one at a time. If you wait, they will build a ring of them, and while you are attacking one, another will be firing at you. If there were Russians there, it was because they chose to be. They should have to take the same chances we take for helping another country.

Anyway, these restrictions were a part of our everyday life, and when I saw a cartoon that seemed to have been created just for us, I had to have it on my wall. We had a sergeant in the outfit who was a truly fine artist, and he drew me the grandest mural of two big vultures sitting on a telephone wire with a caption underneath that read, "Patience, hell, let's go out and kill something!" A hundred visitors had seen that mural, including representatives from the office of the Chairman of the Joint Chiefs, and we never had anything but laughs and good-natured comments about it. Notwithstanding, the mural became history, and soon after, so did I.

My hundred-mission parade was over, the new D/O had arrived, and my orders were official. We had a great party at the club and, with more than just a little reluctance, I tried to say good-bye to a bunch of guys who had flown day after day with me into the most heavily defended areas our Air Force had ever penetrated. We drank too much, made a lot of noise, toasted the guys who didn't make it back, and wobbled back to our trailers to begin all over again the next day. They returned to the heavily-defended areas and I to the Land of the Big BX.

Taxiing out to leave the next afternoon, I found myself musing over the year I spent at Da Nag. The things Bert and I had done to improve the operation before Colonel Maloy arrived; the origination of the Gunfighters; those inspiring, beautifully coordinated complex missions we flew against Hanoi. The pride I always felt in seeing so many units of our Air Force working in perfect harmony to accomplish a single objective is a thing I'll never forget. The rocket attacks, the air-to-air mission for a month or two. The day we lost Norm Gaddis; the circumstances under which we lost Bert and Doug Condit; the midair collision in Pack Six that put my second backseater, Ron Webb, and Lieutenant Colonel Hervey in the Hanoi Hilton for six years. Lance Sijan's incredible effort to survive, Fred Haeffner and the guys from the 390th putting our Gunfighter insignia on the hangar roof, the construction of the squash and racketball building, Sunrise crying as they came to pick up my baggage.

Suddenly I realized we were leveling off. I couldn't even remember getting off the ground. It was with pride, sadness, and not a little frustration that I thought about all the disrupted lives and fatherless kids just in our unit alone. The thought struck me, we should talk longer before we decide to fight, but once there is no other way to go, we should fight with more resolve and less restriction from the civilian side of the house. Considering the ridiculous limits under which we operated at times, I don't see how we could have done any better. I tried to think of my coming assignment to Nellis, but I couldn't push away the faces of the great flyers and young leaders we had that year at Da Nang—Sandy Vandenberg, Sam Baake, Chuck Cunningham, Wayne Elder, Bob Janca, George Sylvester, John Armstrong, Bob Tanguy, Fred Haeffner, Jerry Robbinette, Bob Dilger, Skip Cox, Pat Humphrey, and a host of others. Without them, Da Nang would never have changed from the base I first saw.

★ ★ ★

CHAPTER 20

Nellis—Again!

Nellis was still the great base a few miles north of Las Vegas, but the F-111 was not the kind of assignment a fighter pilot dreamed about. A nightmare maybe; a dream, no.

My good friend Brigadier General Jay Hubbard, who was the commander of Marine Aircraft Group 12 at Chuli, south of Da Nang, had this to say about my F-111 assignment:

"My open and continuous admiration for Boots has only wavered once in over thirty years. That was after our Vietnam tours when I learned that he had accepted an assignment to bombers. I just couldn't believe it. Perhaps his sight or hearing had gone or maybe he had a series of heart attacks. Whatever it was, I had to hear it from him personally, so I popped into Nellis where he worked with the F-111s. He appeared to have the same old bounce and fire. Maybe it was loneliness; that must be it. I decided that Boots had finally chosen to fly with a crowd around—feeding him headings, altitudes, frequencies, coffee, and sandwiches. What a candy ass! Then we went to the flight line where he showed me that big ugly bird with the loose wings. He recounted a recent black-night, low-level mission with the ride set on 'hard.' It scared the hell out of me just listening and I could tell that old Boots was still tactical. I left Nellis just hoping that he'd live long enough to write another book."

Jay and I met when we attended the National War College in 1965 and 1966 and he had a comment or two about that, too. He had found *No Guts, No Glory* very useful during his career, and he commented about our association at the War College:

"Hell, I had felt so indebted to Boots for so many years for writing *No Guts, No Glory,* I would have offered to keep his car washed, golf clubs clean, and caddy for him as well. Fortunately, I never articulated any of that. After getting to know that slick rascal, I have no doubt he would have taken me up on all of it. Now wouldn't a goddamn Air Force type just love to have a Marine orderly!"

Although I said from the start it would be a cold day in hell when I turned my life over to a black box for night all-weather flying at low altitude, three weeks after my checkout in the F-111, I found myself out there in the middle of the night doing just that. There were checks and balances in the TFR (terrain-following radar) system, and once you understood them the mission became more believable. Five hundred knots at 400 feet altitude at night over terrain you can't see is a sporty course any way you look at it, but one day at a time it almost became routine.

The time at Nellis sped by and the operation was going beautifully. At the end of a year I found myself the new commander. I must have given fifty speeches on the F-111 operation during 1969 and 1970. There was controversy, to say the least, over the contract to General Dynamics, so anytime something went wrong, someone suggested cancelling the contract.

The F-111 had problems, but they were resolved and in the final analysis the Air Force more than got its money's worth. It had the only aircraft in the world at that time that could do the night all-weather low-altitude mission automatically.

In December 1969 I got promoted to brigadier general, but I was so busy I hardly noticed. In fact, when John Burns called me from Luke saying we both made it, I was surprised. Other things were on my mind. About three days later we had an accident that set the F-111 program back a couple of years. Six of us were conducting special tests with four aircraft to determine what auxiliary missions the '111 could handle. We did some strafing and low-angle dive-bombing, each of us flying any aircraft set up for the mission.

During the rocket-firing phase an F-111 crew fired, pulled up, and almost immediately a wing came off. The aircraft began rolling just as the crew activated the escape capsule, and consequently there was not enough time for the capsule parachute to open. It could have been any of us, but it really hurt to lose a crew that way.

Extensive investigation proved there was a faulty electronic weld in the wing, and immediately all F-111s were grounded. One aircraft at a time, about eight of us flew every plane back to the plant for a wing inspection. It took over a year and millions of dollars to determine this was a one-of-a-kind accident. Meanwhile, I requested and received from Tactical Air Command seventy-five T-33s to keep our pilots flying. I have often wondered if I would have been promoted had the accident occurred a week earlier.

You have to be lucky if you are going to live through thirty years of flying fighters, and this was certainly one of those times. "Luckier than a two-peckered dog," old Houston Tuel used to say when something good would happen to me. He was adamant about it the day I drew the straw that let me compete in the General Electric race at the 1951 National Air Races. We were at George AFB in the old 94th Hat in the Ring Squadron then.

In the summer of 1970 I was again transferred to George AFB as the air division commander, but I was told I wouldn't be there long. I had two wings under my command, an F-4 training wing at George and a reconnaissance RF-4 wing at Mountain Home, Idaho. I stayed long enough to get both my wing commanders promoted to brigadier general; Hank Warren at Mountain Home and Earl Archer at George—both outstanding pilots and leaders.

★ ★ ★

CHAPTER 21

Vietnam Revisited

In January 1971, I got a call from Air Force Personnel in the Pentagon. I was going back to Vietnam as assistant director of operations for 7th AF in Saigon. My boss was to be Major General Joe Wilson, and there was no hurry as long as I was there by the 15th. I glanced at my calendar; it was 8 January. The family would be allowed several months to find housing. They stayed in Apple Valley nearby.

On the 15th I was shaking hands with Joe Wilson—the beginning of a friendship that remains close after sixteen years. He was an experienced fighter pilot and we got along very well. He was very thorough and patient with me during my transition period, and in a few weeks I was pleased that he trusted me enough to take some leave in Thailand.

General Lucius Clay was Commander 7th Air Force at the time, and Lieutenant General Moose Harden was his deputy. We were a homogeneous group. We got to playing tennis at noon—General Clay, Moose, Joe, and I. One day I was to be Clay's partner, and that bothered me a little because he had a habit of standing in such a way that he blocked part of his partner's serving area. I can still hear Joe telling me, "Don't worry about it. Neither Moose nor I have ever hit him and you won't, either." You guessed it. About the middle of the third game, I uncorked a first serve that hit General Clay right in the back of the head. He wasn't overjoyed at that, but didn't say much, and I thought he took it very well.

The next day the general called me in and notified me I would be going to Quang Tri for about a month to help the Army cut down its helicopter losses. That sounds as though the general was a bit vindictive, but that really wasn't the case. The reason for it surprised us all. I was told a few die-hard senior officers on General Creighton Abrams's staff were trying to prove they needed no help from the Air Force; that they could do their helicopter operations independently. They were constantly running what they called "infil and exfil" operations. The Army would transport Vietnamese soldiers to designated areas in enemy territory where the troops would destroy given objectives, get back in the choppers, and return to base. The problem was, the Army was losing a lot of helos doing this, and with each helo seven or eight soldiers were killed or injured. During some routine questioning, General Abrams, who was Commander, Military Assistance Command, Vietnam, discovered the Air Force was providing no assistance. When he was told the Army hadn't asked for it, he was furious. He contacted General Clay and asked for an Air Force general familiar with air-ground operations to help stop his losses. It was purely a coincidence that my ground-to-ground missile, the tennis ball, was delivered with such unerring accuracy the day before.

Before leaving for Quang Tri, I attended a meeting with General Abrams and the personnel responsible for the helicopter operation. I never heard such terms of negative endearment. I mean General Abrams was mad. He gave me complete authority over the entire infil/exfil operation to conduct matters as I saw fit. That went over like an iron balloon with the Army group. It also laid a great responsibility on me, because, at the time, I hadn't the foggiest idea of what I was going to do to correct the situation.

I got the Army to give me a briefing on what they wanted to do and how they were doing it. Their briefing included the fact that Air Force response to their request for air support took thirty to forty minutes, and by then it was too late. A good point if there is no prior planning.

Armed with the fact that response time had to be improved and the infil/exfil teams had to be protected in some way, I packed my bags and headed for Quang Tri. On arrival I found myself actually working for General Lahm, the Vietnamese commander of I Corps. He had several other recently appointed advisers, but as his air adviser, I got a lot of attention. It was General Lahm's practice to hold his staff meeting each evening at Khe Sanh, where more of his field commanders were available. That meant every afternoon I boarded a helicopter and headed across enemy territory to Khe Sanh. The "nap-of-the-earth" concept had already been born, so each evening we traveled that thirty minutes or so at treetop altitude. We used to get hit at 600 knots in the Hanoi area in F-4s, so traveling at low altitude at 95 or 100 knots left me with a very insecure feeling.

A review of the Army problem brought to mind several ideas, but the one I liked the best was establishing corridors. I didn't have enough air support to cover the whole area in which the Army worked, but if they all went to and from their targets using established corridors, I could defend that. By working over the corridors ahead of time with fighter support, and using B-52s to bomb the landing areas, losses were cut to almost zero immediately. That left only the problem of too long a response when the Army called for help. To improve that situation, I created what became known as our "fire hose" system. We had fighter aircraft on alert, we had an airborne C-130 who remained in contact with the Army at all times, and we had the Army units who wanted help. Instead of waiting for the Army to call, I established an airborne fighter alert where the flight leader circled with his aircraft until given a target. When called, the fighters responded in two to three minutes and the Army was delighted. The problem was when they were *not* called. The aircraft had to return to base and land with munitions aboard or in some cases jettison their loads in the water if tricky winds or bad weather existed. In any event, it worked well and was preferable to a system that left a unit without air support when really needed.

We continued to travel each evening to Khe Sanh, where we learned what was expected in the way of support for the next two days. On the way over one late afternoon, two helicopters flying nap-of-the-earth were suddenly surprised by considerable fire from the North Vietnamese. One helo was hit and went down. The other, which I was in, circled for a minute or so and then landed to pick up the passengers and crew. As soon as we touched down, a crewman tossed me a carbine and, pointing to the edge of the clearing, shouted, "Cover us from there!" I jumped out and ran thirty or forty yards and found some concealment. I didn't mind observing, but I didn't want to be observed in the process. Three other officers were on the other sides of the chopper doing the same thing. I couldn't help thinking how ironic it would be, after all the combat missions I had flown, to get hit or captured screwing around on the ground during a helicopter rescue mission. An Air Force general—a fighter pilot—with a rifle! The rescue didn't take but a couple of minutes and soon we were on the way to Khe Sanh again. This time in an overloaded chopper, flying nap-of-the-earth.

It was an interesting month I spent at Quang Tri. We had large tents that provided three or four of us ample space for the few things we brought with us. The tents had a wooden base about three or four feet up, while the canvas tent closed the space above. We were carefully briefed not to wander around after dark, since attacks had been made on the camp recently. I guess, just so I wouldn't miss anything, the Vietcong scheduled one the last week I was there. I was coming back from the latrine when I heard a single shot fired, soon followed by a dozen or so. I raced back to my tent just in time to avoid more shots and a bunch of people running through the tent area. A couple of tents away, I heard automatic rifle fire as the VC sprayed a couple of people there. I grabbed my carbine and jammed a magazine in it. Another clip went into a .45 I pulled out of my duffel bag. I didn't know where my tentmates were, but right then I was wishing someone was around—anyone. Voices, people running, more shots—I sunk to the floor on the side away from the door and propped myself up against the wooden post of the tent. I held the carbine and set the pistol on the floor next to me. One thing was certain as far as I was concerned—I wasn't going alone. The first one through that door was going with me. The confusion continued for a few more minutes. Then, as quickly as it started, it was over. Soon everyone was around talking. A couple of them and a couple of our people were killed and that was it. The rest of the time at Quang Tri, I was jumpy. I guess I just became aware of how quickly things could change on the ground. Anyway, a week later I was back in Saigon playing tennis again at noon. After that month, I developed a high lob serve.

I enjoyed getting back to my trailer again. Each general officer had an aide to take care of the trailer and cook his meals. It was like having a wife (except for one important detail!). Master Sergeant Bennie Mills was my aide and he was an absolute delight. Smart and capable, he knew his job to the last detail, and sometimes I suspected he knew mine at least as well as I did.

In May I received some really bad news. My wife had to have an immediate cancer operation. I spent about a month in the States and then, when she was on her feet again, I headed back to Saigon. On arrival, I learned General Clay was going to become PacAF commander at Hickam AFB, Hawaii. Because of Dotty's condition, I also got orders to Hickam to become the assistant director of operations for PacAF. After just enough time back in Saigon to let Joe Wilson have a couple of weeks off, I headed for Hawaii.

★ ★ ★

CHAPTER 22

The Good Life

I spent about six months as assistant DO, got promoted to major general, and became the deputy for operations. It was a good job. Everyone in the headquarters felt we were really running the war in Southeast Asia. Actually, it was more like the story of the 100,000 ants on the log floating downstream, each ant dead sure he had ahold of the rudder.

I was just settling in at Hickam AFB, Hawaii (PacAF Headquarters), when my brother-in-law, Colonel Aubrey Bobbitt, died at Clark AFB in the Philippines. I rushed out there to help my sister through a very rough period and then, together, we brought him to Arlington National Cemetery for burial. "Bunny" was a magnificent guy and his death ended a lot of long-talked-over plans as to what we were going to do after retirement.

When General Clay became PacAF commander, he brought Joe Wilson and Moose Harden with him, the same team we had in Saigon. I didn't really enjoy working for General Clay, although he was a very bright, inquisitive person. He wasn't too experienced in the fighter world, and I soon found myself going in with one briefing and coming out with two more on relatively insignificant subjects. I made decisions on my own to avoid additional briefings and, at times, had to account for those decisions. It wasn't the way to be a good staff officer, but I'm afraid I'd do it that way again if I had it to do over.

Lucius Clay seemed to delight in pointing out that I had never served in the Pentagon, where he had about seventeen years' experience. The third or fourth time that occurred, we were at a party and I foolishly told him I had been too busy with the primary mission of the Air Force, "to fly and fight," to get involved in secondary missions. It had just the effect you would suspect and, though I knew I had just lost the war, it felt great to win one battle.

PacAF was a good assignment, and the two years I spent in Hawaii were gone with the speed of light. We accomplished a few things; most notably we got the F-111 and the A-7 into combat.

I had some of my ops planners working on how to get out of Vietnam when and if the time came, and the F-111 and A-7 became part of the solution. I was sure of one thing: if we kept all the tankers out there, we could never close up enough bases. We needed to keep the pressure on North Vietnam, which then was done with F-4s and F-105s using tankers for additional fuel every time we hit a target.

It seemed to me the F-111 and the A-7 were exactly what was needed. Both aircraft could strike targets around Hanoi without refueling, which meant that for the first time since the war began, we could actually strike with surprise. Those two kinds of aircraft could keep the pressure on North Vietnam while practically everything else in the theater went home. It was a natural and, after several briefings and a little help from the Pentagon, we made it happen. With a rough spot or two operationally, it worked out as we planned and provided us with viable options time after time as we began to withdraw our forces.

Another of my efforts at PacAF was to try to get the people in the combat zone to use the gun on the F-4. After all the effort we expended at Da Nang in 1967 to show the advantages of having both missiles and guns on the aircraft, five years later we were still confronted with relatively senior personnel who lacked the background or experience in aerial combat to understand the problem. When they were captains and not yet dry behind the ears, we were educating people that guns and missiles are complementary weapons—they do not compete with each other. We taught that at the Fighter Weapons School at Nellis as far back as 1957. It took some attention from the chief of staff and the commander of PacAF, but finally Phantoms with both missiles and guns began to show up in the air-to-air fights again. During the Vietnam War, where contacts with enemy aircraft were infrequent, sixteen MiGs were shot down by the F-4's gun, so the principle must have had some merit even to the nonbelievers.

★ ★ ★

CHAPTER 23

The Puzzle Palace

In the fall of 1973 I suddenly got orders to the Pentagon. I was given about twenty-five Army, Navy, and Air Force personnel and told to go to Israel to evaluate all the weapons and equipment we gave the Israelis to fight the Yom Kippur War. We evaluated everything possible—guns, tanks, air-to-air missiles, aircraft, hospital equipment, ground-to-air missiles, chemical-warfare equipment, and dozens of other things.

While I was there, the chief of staff of the Israeli Air Force General Peled asked me to visit some of his fighter squadrons and discuss air-to-air combat. I don't know how much they learned, but I certainly learned a lot. I came out of Israel with a healthy respect for an air force that was small but probably the most efficient in the world. I had a Israeli counterpart, General Uzi Elam, who had a team similar to mine with parallel objectives. Working with him was a delight and we became good friends in the process of accomplishing our two government missions. We traveled all over Israel, parts of Syria, and even visited a captured SA-2 surface-to-air missile site in Egypt. That was especially interesting to me, since it was the same SAM we dodged in Vietnam so often six years before.

Soon our mission was complete, and with our volumes of information surrendered to government officials, we all got new assignments.

In July 1974 I became deputy inspector general of the Air Force, working for Lieutenant General Don Nunn. Don and I got along great and I enjoyed working for him. I never had a job I couldn't become interested in, but I was approaching age fifty-five and had some important decisions to make. You had to be able to give industry ten years if you wanted to work after retirement, and mandatory retirement age in industry was sixty-five. That meant you better get out by age fifty-five and that's exactly what I decided to do. So with twenty-nine years, nine months service, I decided to hang it up and went to work for Grumman Corporation in Washington, D.C.

When my retirement plans from the Air Force were announced, I began receiving letters and telegrams from people I had known through the years. I guess there must have been sixty or seventy in all. It made me feel the same way I did the day I punched out of the F-86 in Korea—all the guys saying something encouraging just before I ejected. Some were funny, others very sincere, but all found a very receptive old fighter pilot grateful for the good luck he had enjoyed all those years and for the friends he made along the way.

CHAPTER 24

The Right Stuff

Retirement from the Air Force means different things to different people—to me it meant a new career, new friends, and new objectives in life. To my first wife it meant other things—not wrong things, just different ones. We separated in October 1978, bought separate houses, and chose different roads to travel.

One of my roads led to being a member and later president of the American Fighter Aces Association. In that capacity, I had received an invitation to the Thunderbird reunion to be held in Las Vegas, Nevada, 20–23 November 1980. With Betty, who became my second wife, I decided to go, and made plans to stay at the MGM Hotel because an ex–Air Force friend, Boots Boothby, was a hotel executive there.

We had a good trip to Las Vegas, rented a car, made arrangements to see a midnight show, and went to the MGM to get our things unpacked. The show was good, but because I had a nine o'clock golf game, we didn't hang around long after it was over. By 0300 we were down for the count.

The next thing I knew, I was hearing the words, "Honey, wake up, wake up. I smell smoke!" coming from another world somewhere. I opened my eyes and found they were burning already. Betty sure as hell did smell smoke. It was 0755. My mind went from sound asleep to processing a hundred thoughts a second. I jumped out of bed and ran to open the door to see what the situation was in the hallway. As I opened the door, a wall of acrid black smoke pushed its way in. I slammed the door and yelled to Betty, "Honey, get on the horn and see what's going on. We have a hell of a problem up here!"

"I already did that," she said, "and the lines are dead."

That statement signaled the beginning of the longest three hours I think I have ever spent. I began stuffing towels around the door to stop the smoke from flowing in but gave that up. Smoke was also coming in through the air-conditioning vents and seeping in around the electrical fixtures. Betty and I went out on the small balcony we had, which was about six feet by twenty feet in area. The parking lot was empty and in a few seconds I counted eight or nine helicopters all coming and going in the process apparently of taking fire fighters to the roof. One thing was certain—this was no drill. Betty said she had checked and knew the fire escape was only a hundred feet or so outside our door. The hallway was filled with smoke and so dark you couldn't even read the door numbers.

"If we try for the fire escape and it's filled with smoke, the ball game's over. I think we should wait it out till we see fire in the room and then, as a last resort, it's wet sheets over our heads and a try for the fire escape."

Betty didn't argue, and the two of us began a series of routine chores to ensure we gave ourselves the best chance of survival.

"Look around for anything that holds water," I suggested. "Fill it and put it out on the balcony, it may come in handy."

I moved a bowl of fruit to the balcony—not bad, food and water. A couple of small chairs seemed like a good idea. Betty was busily stripping the bed, throwing the sheets in the bathtub, which she filled up. She then rolled the dripping sheets in a ball and put them on the balcony. The smoke continued to roll in—we were barely able to see across the room.

We kept checking outside. We had a commanding view of

everything going on because the building was L shaped where we were and there was only one floor above us. Far below we saw chairs, couches, and other heavy objects fly through windows and hurtle to the ground. If you had no balcony, you had no air. We could see people lying on their stomachs trying to hit a happy medium between getting some air and falling out the window. One couple, deathly afraid of fire, calmly stepped off the balcony and plunged to their deaths. Later, a man tumbled to his death when he lost his grip on the bed sheets he had tied together to fashion his escape. We were running out of things to do to improve our situation, so I handed Betty one of our cameras and said, "Take some pictures. You'll love 'em when we get out of all this." Without batting an eye, Betty began snapping shot after shot depicting our deteriorating situation. The opposite side of the building, which we could see so well initially, was now barely visible and smoke was pouring from new places near the roof.

Why, I don't know, but I suddenly turned to Betty and said, "Betty, you have as much common sense as I do, and you can see this situation is at best a toss-up. If we get out of this, it will be with whatever we have on. Go in the room and put on the dress you like the best; when you're finished, I'll get dressed up too. If we make it out of here, we'll have something to wear to the Thunderbird reunion—if we don't, at least we'll go out first class."

I thought later how dumb that was to say something like that—it certainly didn't sound too encouraging. It didn't seem to matter to her at the time, however, because in less than a second I got a thumbs-up from her and she disappeared into the smoke-filled room. A minute or two later she reappeared in a wine-colored ultrasuede dress and high heels—and a face covered with soot. I couldn't help laughing at her—she was a bum in a tuxedo if I had ever seen one. I grabbed one of our wet cloths and wiped her face clean. "Stick out your tongue," I said. "Let's see what your throat looks like."

It was coated black as far as I could see, so from then on we made it a point every fifteen minutes or so to wipe out the inside of our mouths and noses. I took my turn inside and came out with black trousers, gray ultrasuede coat, white shirt, and red and black tie. There we were, dressed for a cocktail party, standing on the twenty-fifth floor balcony, smoke all around us, not knowing if we were going to be alive or dead in the next half hour.

We heard the couple on a balcony two or three rooms away call to us to ask what we were going to do. I told them we were sitting tight until we saw fire in the room and then it was the last-resort dash to the fire exit. They said they were going for the exit now and wished us good luck. It was they who needed the good luck—they were found dead propped up against the wall in the hallway—out of air and unable to find the exit in the dense smoke.

Things continued to get worse and I found myself wondering how this was all going to turn out. As if to keep me from coming to any conclusion, subconsciously I began thinking of things I could do—and things Betty could do to keep her occupied. I decided it was a good idea to move all our clothes to the balcony. We agreed that one at a time we would race into the room, grab what we could, and return. When twenty seconds had elapsed, it would be presumed there was trouble and the other would come to help. Visibility at this stage was about six feet in the room. As soon as we had moved all the clothes out and stacked them neatly on the balcony, I told Betty to go in and go to the bathroom. She shot me an unbelieving glance and gracefully declined. "Go on, Betty, whether you think you need to or not—in another ten minutes you won't be able to." Off she went, disappearing into the smoke to return a minute or two later with a look of "How did you know" on her face. I followed suit—and on the way out, more out of curiosity than anything else, I flipped on the TV set. Where the electricity came from I'll never know, but that TV set was soon bringing one of the morning news stations into our very private world. Suddenly we heard, "We interrupt this program to bring you the following announcement: There is a major fire in the MGM Hotel in Las Vegas, Nevada, and all the occupants above the eighteenth floor are hopelessly trapped." Betty commented, "We already know that."

By this time I had my face a foot or two from the screen and found myself watching our hotel with flames and smoke pouring from the lower stories of the building. I could plainly see our room at the top, which made me feel like I was at the end of a closed circle. It was a strange feeling.

By this time we had two chairs, fruit, wet towels, all our clothes, two cameras, wet sheets, and as many containers full of water that we could find all out on the balcony. We were set to wait it out. Betty was marvelous, outwardly calm and very efficient about doing whatever I suggested. It was better having her there than another fighter pilot—he would have argued about everything.

My tee time came and went. The golfers at Paradise Valley were getting impatient, so Jimmy Johnson, one of the foursome, called the hotel to see if I had left. A very heroic telephone operator, who was still doing her duty long after she should have left, told him to look out the window—the MGM was on fire. Jimmy dropped the golf club and headed for the MGM looking for us. It was an all-day job that took him to the hotel, hospitals, rescue centers, and the convention center, all without success. In desperation, at his last stop near the hotel, he asked a policeman. The policeman suggested several places to look but Jimmy had already been there. The cop then suggested he check the morgue, indicating the count of dead (which eventually went to eighty-four) was past fifty already. Jimmy was a double ace and wing commander in Korea. He expressed himself forcibly:

"Morgue?" he shouted. "I'm not checking any goddamn morgue. If one guy gets out of that hotel alive, it will be him!"

Jimmy started back to his car which was parked a couple of blocks away in a lot belonging to the Continental Motel.

Betty and I continued to wait it out. The smoke was too thick to consider entering the room for any reason, so we were now on the balcony for the duration. I told Betty not to worry—to think of all the stories she could tell about the fire when we got back. I reminded her they had rescue equipment at Nellis AFB. I knew because we had it ten years before, when I was commander there. Eventually they would come for those left on the balconies.

The smoke was now coming up from the room below, curling up over our balcony from underneath. The wind kept us moving from side to side. We were like tigers in a cage moving back and forth in what was a vain effort to get away from the smoke.

Suddenly from around the corner of the building, an Air Force helicopter appeared. He hovered as close to us as he could get—maybe thirty or forty feet from the balcony. To say I was glad to see him would be the understatement of my life. I wanted to tell him I was Air Force, that I was familiar with his rescue equipment, and that to say the least, we would welcome his help. All I could think of was a good old Air Force universal greeting—I stood at attention with jacket and tie whipping in his generated windstorm and gave him the best salute I could render. He gave me a thumbs-up and departed. Watching him leave, I couldn't help wondering what he thought my salute meant. A minute or two later another chopper appeared above us and we saw an airman on a penetrator descending toward us. The penetrator was used in Vietnam to get through the tree cover and pick up downed airmen. It was like a piece of flagpole coming down, but the person to be picked up could pull out a small section at the end to sit on. No straps, just a place to sit. You were expected to wrap your arms around the vertical part of the pole for the million-dollar ride. As the airman got close to us, he was unable to drop to the balcony because of an overhang on the floor above. He hung at our level seven or eight feet away and, while holding on with one hand, he began to uncoil a rope he had on his belt. He made several unsuccessful attempts to toss me the rope, but finally I caught it and began pulling him over to the balcony.

Just as he was getting close to the wrought-iron railing that bordered the balcony, the chopper dropped down, jerking him partially off the penetrator. I wrapped my right leg around one of the vertical poles of the railing, leaned over, and shot my arm under the straps of his safety harness. I had him, but I couldn't move him over the railing. His weight plus the weight of the penetrator was just too much. Betty made a grab for the leg of his flight suit and brought him over close to the railing. That did it. He was able to get one leg over the railing and soon we had him on the balcony floor. For a moment he just sat there, then he slowly and deliberately raised himself to the standing position. He looked over at me as he dusted off his flight suit and said, "Jesus Christ, I was having a hard time figuring out who was saving who out there!"

Betty, all this time, was thinking he would now pull out a Scottpack or mask of some type that would allow us to make it to the roof. Instead, he began motioning to Betty to sit on the penetrator. The chopper was noisy, the wind was blowing everything around, and it was difficult to hear, but I heard Betty say, "Me, on that damn thing? You must be out of your mind!" That was her only negative thought. After that she was listening intently to what he had to say. The penetrator was a piece of equipment that required some practice to use safely. Fighter pilots got instruction on its use during their combat-crew training en route to Southeast Asia. Betty getting on that thing with a forty-five-second briefing left me tight-jawed, but the thought of burning up in that hotel wasn't too good either. She was about ready, and above the wind and chopper noise I wanted to tell her not to reach out when she was being helped into the chopper. It was too noisy, but I shouted into her ear, "Can you hear me?" Her head bounced back and forth indicating she could. "No matter what happens," I shouted, "don't let go. Understand?" Again her head indicating okay. Her eyes, wide open and understandably laced with some fear, reminded me of the painting of the little French girl with the saucerlike eyes. "Honey," she blurted out, "I'm not having a very good time." At that we released her and off the twenty-fifth-floor balcony she sailed. Because of the overhang, she was gone in an instant. When we next saw her she was above the twenty-sixth floor and being drawn up toward the chopper. After that I couldn't see her. I just watched out over the balcony and prayed I didn't see her go by on the way down. A few minutes later the penetrator was back, but, as before, it was hanging out away from the balcony. Using the radio, the airman got the pilot to move the helicopter so as to make the penetrator sway back and forth until we could grab it. We talked about who should go next, because this was all new to him also. I suggested he go since I was "penetrator-trained,"so to speak, and felt I could do it alone. "Christ, no!" he said. "The pilot would kill me if I left you down here by yourself." We compromised. I would go next, but I would do it alone so the airman could learn from my mistakes. I got on the little four-inch ledge outside of the wrought-iron railing and looped one arm under and around the horizontal part of the railing. With the left arm I tried to stabilize the penetrator, which was moving up and down and left and right a little as the helicopter moved. I crouched and got ready to get on the penetrator but it was an elusive target. Each time I was about to drop onto it, the penetrator would move. It had to be just right—I had to drop on the horizontal part, which would be my seat, but at the same time it was necessary to let go of the railing and get both arms around the vertical part before I slipped off the seat. After three "almosts," I can remember smiling inwardly and saying to myself, "Boots, it's like a three-foot putt; you won't know the result until you give it a go." At that I dropped onto the seat part, let go of the railing, and grabbed for the pole. I hit the horizontal bar off center, which was probably good—I never did like soprano voices on older men. With my arm around the vertical part, I was able to straighten myself up. It seemed to me that all happened in a split second, but when I was able to look around I found myself 150 feet or so away from the building. That was the slingshot effect caused by routing the cable on the overhang above us. The thought kept coming back to me that Betty had just done this. How did she pull it off? This was a sporty course to say the least—In fact, it scared the hell out of me if the truth were known.

They began reeling me up toward the chopper, and things were looking good until I got about twenty-five feet or so underneath. Suddenly I began to spin, slowly at first but increasing to the point where I had to get the upper part of my body closer to the vertical pole to keep from being pulled away. It took all the strength I had to overcome that centrifugal force and again I wondered how Betty was able to handle all this. Finally, they pulled me inside the chopper, but I was so dizzy I just sat there for a minute or two to regain my bearings. I asked Betty about her trip up and she said she didn't spin like that. She told me she thought I was out of my mind when I said don't let go. What idiot would do that? But later as she approached the chopper, an airman who was buckled to the aircraft leaned way out to grab a strap under her. She started to reach out to him and then thought, This is what he meant by don't let go no matter what.

We lost several pilots in Vietnam who got all the way to the open door of the chopper and then loosened their grip on the penetrator to grab an extended hand. The chopper lurched, and back down into the water the pilot went, only now soaking wet and falling from a hundred feet or so. He couldn't get back to the surface. It's a heartbreaking experience to come that close to a successful save and then lose a man. In our case, the fall from twenty-five floors wouldn't have hurt us, but the sudden stop at the end would have ruined the whole day.

The penetrator was already on its way back down before I could get my seat belt buckled in the chopper. Soon the airman was back safely and the pilot flew to the south side of the hotel to let us off. Betty, trying to get down that rope ladder with her high heels on, was a sight to behold. She eventually fell into the airman's arms at the bottom, so he saved her a second time. The chopper sped off blowing dust and sand all over the place.

We couldn't have cared less, we were to glad to know it was all over.

We headed for an aid station which was pointed out to us and eventually were taken over to the convention center, which was being used as a central gathering point for survivors. We gave our names to several officials, but for some reason, we never appeared on any survivor lists. Betty was cold, so I got some blankets and a cot and let her lie down for a little while. They were passing out food, so I got myself a sandwich and something to drink and went back to take care of Betty. She was okay in a few minutes so we reported in officially and were assigned a room at the Continental Motel (ground floor) a few blocks away from the MGM. It was about noon. The room was fine. We didn't have anything but the clothes on our backs so we decided to go to a drugstore and get a few essentials. We walked out of the motel around the corner of the building and literally bumped smack into Jimmy Johnson. Jimmy had about given up on us and was heading for his car in the parking lot, so the collision was something to behold. He threw his arms around both of us and the three of us hugged and let the teardrops roll—which they did. We went to Jimmy's house and he, his wife Sylvia, Betty, and I sat around drinking screwdrivers for the better part of the afternoon celebrating the fact that we had cheated the grim reaper once more.

At six we were back at the motel. Betty and I had decided that maybe we better show up at the cocktail party—everyone knew we were at the MGM, and so at least all our friends would know we were alive and well. When I first suggested it Betty pleaded, "Give me a break. This has been a long day." But after a promise that we would stay no longer than a half hour, she was all for it. We cleaned up the best we could, but anyone within a four-dollar ride in a taxi could smell the smoke in our clothes.

The party was at Caesars Palace—a beautiful spread of food in the middle of a very large room with tables all around. Betty and I strolled over to one of the tables, but before we could even sit down, a couple of fighter pilots that we knew came over to congratulate us on our very fortunate escape. A question or two, then another—more people gathered around us asking questions of both Betty and I. Soon there was a complete circle around us and we found ourselves answering one question after another. It was then I noticed that most of the fighter pilots were intrigued with Betty and her actions. Most of them had been on the penetrator and had an appreciation for what she had been through. The fact that she was very pretty didn't discourage them either. I noticed the circle swinging more her way—Betty noticed it too, because several times she brought me into her description of events and was met with, "We knew Boots would make it, never mind him. What did you do next?" Well, our half-hour deadline had come and gone and there was Betty in the middle of the circle, excitedly recalling our actions during the day. By now I was part of the crowd—observing, listening, thinking about everything that had happened that 21st day of November 1980. There was Betty, I mused. How magnificent she had been. All my life I had thought only fighter pilots, race drivers, test pilots, and people like that had the guts for the type of life I had led these past thirty years or so. But here was a gal with three kids, too busy during her life for athletics and competitive games, who finds herself faced with death and gives not so much as a whimper from fear. No "Why mes?" no "What about the kids?" just "What do I do next?" She gets a thirty-second briefing on a device she has never seen before and allows herself to be pushed off a balcony on the twenty-fifth floor of a burning hotel. If that isn't a person who has whatever it takes, I guess I'll just have to wait till the next life to find one.

Epilogue

During the process of telling my story, I introduced you to many people whose lives helped shape my own. It seems less than fair to let them disappear without your knowing how they fared through the years.

Kay, my first serious love in the Philippines, married an outstanding young officer who rose to the rank of major general (two stars) in the Air Force. They raised a wonderful family and she is now living in California.

Lila Lee, my beautiful cousin, married as fine a guy as you would ever want to meet. They have lived like millionaires for the past thirty-five years in New Orleans, and at this writing they are vacationing in Europe.

My longtime friend, War College classmate, and Vietnam combat associate Jay Hubbard retired from the Marine Corps as a brigadier. He moved to California, and you'll never find a more dedicated, loyal American.

Gabby Gabreski, my wing commander at Selfridge, my competitor in Korea, and my lifelong friend, became the U.S. Air Force's leading living ace. He retired a full colonel, then worked almost twenty years for Grumman Corporation in New York. He is now retired on Long Island.

Colonel Harry Thyng, my wing commander who became a jet ace in Korea, returned to the States and retired as a brigadier general. He later ran for Congress but missed being elected by a precious few votes. A fighter ace in two wars, he died in 1983 widely admired and respected by those who knew him.

Bud Mahurin, the Boy Colonel, got out of the Air Force after his release from prison camp in Korea. He works for an aviation company in California and still looks like he's about forty years young.

My group commander at Nellis in 1955, Bruce Hinton, retired as a full colonel and has worked for Hughes Corporation ever since.

Chick Cleveland, the young lieutenant in Korea who became "the Ivory Ace," retired from the Air Force with three stars and lives in Montgomery, Alabama.

Earl Brown—"Brownie"—my friend of thirty-seven years who was my cool, gutsy, capable wingman in Korea, rose to lieutenant general. He may be the only three-star ski instructor in Pennsylvania these days.

John Taylor, the original old soldier and my right arm at Soesterberg, retired from the Air Force a lieutenant colonel and is living in Homestead, Florida.

Bill Yancey, the operations officer for whom I fought and who served me so well at Soesterberg, retired as a major general and now works for a real-estate company in Springfield, Virginia.

I am happy to say that Boom Boom and I remain friends. He also retired a major general and lives in northern Florida.

My handball-racketball partner at Da Nang, Bob Tanguy of the 480th Fighter Squadron, is another two-star retiree. He lives on a wooded estate in Indiana and he calls occasionally to see how things are. The first words I always hear are "You bastard . . ."

Fred Haeffner, jack of all trades, the driving force behind my wing weapons section and later the 390th Fighter Squadron commander at Da Nang, retired as a major general 30 September 1987. He is working for Lockheed and living in California.

"Sunrise" probably still lives in the suburbs of Da Nang, where her children will be raised under communism.

Dotty, my first wife, settled in Arlington, Virginia, and is remodeling an older house—something she said she always wanted to do.

Robin Olds, combat leader extraordinaire in World War II and Vietnam, retired a brigadier general. He moved to Steamboat Springs and spends his days skiing the slopes of the Colorado mountains.

Christine. After a number of years Christine married again, this time to an old high-school acquaintance. They are living in California, and I hope she is as happily married as I am.

Me? After twenty-eight years of flying fighters and two years in the Pentagon, I bid the good ole Air Force good-bye and went to work for Grumman Corporation in Washington, D.C. In 1986 I retired from Grumman, and Betty and I moved to Melbourne, Florida, where we built a home in a thirty-six-hole golfing community. Though I have a couple of consulting jobs, most of my time is dedicated to getting my handicap from three to scratch. I'm going to do it if it kills me—what a way to go!

About the Author

Major General F. C. Blesse, USAF (Ret.), is best known as the author of the classic fighter tactics manual *No Guts, No Glory*. He is also known as "Boots," the childhood nickname that became his lifelong moniker. Now, in his exciting, honest memoir, he fills in the rest of the story of a professional fighter pilot's eventful life.

Born into an Army family in the Panama Canal Zone in 1921, Boots Blesse graduated from West Point in 1945 and spent twenty-eight of the next thirty years in fighter aircraft. He flew two tours in Korea, becoming the nation's sixth-ranking jet ace, and returned to combat over Vietnam. In all, he has flown 380 combat missions and holds thirty-six decorations.

In *"Check Six"* Blesse recounts his life from West Point to his position as Deputy Inspector General of the Air Force. Nothing is held back as Blesse describes in detail his full story from the ground up—the triumphs, failures, challenges, and luck that played a part in his career.